WOW!

Scammed or Not Scammed!

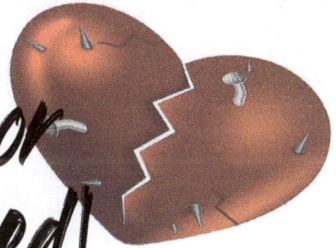

WOW!

Scammed or Not Scammed!

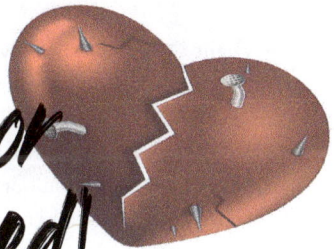

by

BEVERLY KORIBANIC

ARPress

ILLUMINATING IDEAS.
EMPOWERING VOICES

ARPress LLC
45 Dan Road Suite 5
Canton MA 02021
Hotline: 1(888) 821-0229
Fax: 1(508) 545-7580

Ordering Information:
Quantity sales. Special discounts are available on quantity purchases by corporations, associations, and others. For details, contact the publisher at the address above.

Printed in the United States of America.

ISBN-13:	Softcover	979-8-89330-398-8
	eBook	979-8-89330-399-5

Library of Congress Control Number: 2024900781

Contents

CHAPTER 1

START OF AN INCREDIBLE ADVENTURE 1

CHAPTER 2

SCAMMER NUMBER TWO 35

CHAPTER 3

WAKE-UP CALL. 44

CHAPTER 4

HARD REALIZATION 48

CHAPTER 5

TRYING TO SCAM Å SCAMMER 51

CHAPTER 6

FEELING STUPID AFTER FINALLY
REALIZING WHAT ACTUALLY
OCCURRED AND HOW IT
OCCURRED. 62

CHAPTER 7

FINALLY MEETING OTHERS
WHO WERE ALSO SCAMMED. 67

CHAPTER 8

MOVING ON. 80

CHAPTER 9

HARD LESSON LEARNED 83

CHAPTER 10

GOVERNMENT AGENCIES
FOR FILING COMPLAINTS .88

CHAPTER 11

SYNOPSIS 92

CHAPTER 12

LAST CHAPTER 103

PREFACE

I AM IN REAL estate, which basically means I use social media to communicate. It is an integral part of my job. It keeps me in-touch with my past and current clients. It is also a means for future clients. Without social media, my business would drop, and people would eventually forget who I am and what I do.

With that being said, I am going to try and warn you about some of the pitfalls of social media. Nothing is perfect. I was scammed, and as of this writing it is still going on. I am hoping that some of the official departments that handle these issues kick in, but as of this writing, no one has addressed this issue.

In this book, I am hoping to address the following:

Item 1) If you think you are being scammed, guess you guessed right. Quit doing whatever you are doing and move on. I should have done this but got caught up in the drama. There can be lots of emotions that you will feel when you are being scammed, whatever the scam may be. Whether you are male or female, it doesn't matter. My story that I am going to tell you happened to me, and the scammer was male.

Item 2) You start an innocent conversation (for you, it is innocent; for the scammer, it is his prelude to something you never in your life would guess you would be intrigued by—yes, I said intrigued). It will appear that you are in a story that was written by somebody with quite an imagination, and every day you go through another chapter of intrigue. This can be horrifying at times. Plus, I added Item 3 below, which is:

Item 3) ROMANCE—because there is a lot of romance to being scammed. OH, YES, there is. The romance is beyond belief. All your senses will be engaged. You will find that you will want this person romantically in the worst way. They say everything right. We all want to find that perfect person who romances us. We buy the songs and sing the songs of romance and love. We buy and read the books of romance and love. We read poetry of romance and love. But when it actually comes to practicing and actually living the life of romance, we sadly fall short in a BIG way. We all start off by wining and dining, as well as surprising our date, our love, our significant other, or spouse with gifts, cards, letters/ notes, etc. However, over time this sometimes (not always) dies. When it dies, it never comes back to life. Sad, but it is true. Then the scammer comes along, who brings all the feelings you thought were dead down deep inside back to life. For me—and I can only speak for me—I found the me I had forgotten. I found the me that I used to be. Was finding me worth all I went through? The jury is still out on that one. The scammer will find what makes you tick, so to speak, and they prey on it like a leopard sitting in a tree, waiting for the next kill.

Item 4) What would life be if we didn't blame others for our own stupidity? It isn't what the scammer did to you. It is what you did to yourself. No one held a gun to your head. They aren't even in the same state or country as you. Feels kinda like getting a divorce or having a breakup with a longstanding partner, but you never had any of the perks that go along with marriage. I think that is the worst part. There isn't much difference because you are in love (very much so), and then you get jilted or burned. However, the timespan is so much quicker. You live a lifetime in what seems forever in such a short time span. It is very hard to explain, but hopefully when reading my story, you will come to understand.

I never considered myself desperate for love or affection. I did not join a dating service when this happened. I wasn't looking for love. I wasn't looking for anything. I never had an issue getting a date. I had joined dating services in the past because I thought they would weed out the bizarre and absurd, but they really don't. I consider myself logical. At the very least, I like to think I am logical. I think I am somewhat intelligent. I am a lover of life, of children, of all animals. I love romance. I definitely love romance. It is not unusual for me to get stopped wherever I am and have people I don't know talk to me or for children to walk up to me or even animals to wander over to me. I have had people hug and kiss me who only met me for about a half-hour.

Some will tell me their life story when we first meet. In fact, some will look at me and cry and tell me their hardship story in the first meeting. I know this is not the norm, but I do not think of it as out of the ordinary because for me, it isn't. So having someone I don't know contact me through Facebook or other media is normal for me, and for them to say "HI" and start a conversation is also normal. Plus, my profession doesn't help me much since I am a real estate agent, as I mentioned earlier, and I get contacted quite frequently by people who are out of state or out of the country and want to converse. I have been independent my entire life and never depended on anyone for support...

However, I fell into a web and got caught up in it, where it truly seemed like reality because it was too bizarre not to be real. Who in the world would make up this kind of story for the sake of the almighty dollar? The sad part is that it happens quite a bit to a lot of people. Is it an addiction? In some respect, I would say yes, because you are so caught up in helping them that you get lost a little, and sometimes you really can't see the forest for the trees, so to speak. This part is very hard to explain unless you have been scammed because it does seem and feel real. Your feelings are truly involved and fully engaged. You feel like an integral part of their lives.

The sad part is the scamming goes unnoticed by so many people. Some don't even know they are being scammed. PLUS, people also think, *This will never happen to me*. SURPRISE! It can and does happen to many people who thought the same thing. Is there help? No, not really. This is the sad part. The organizations that are supposed to help drag their feet so the person or persons doing the scamming has/have time to change their name, picture, ID, or web videos—yes, I said web videos. Through reading the scamming articles, many people are scammed by looking at the person (scammer) who was seen on a web cam to find out that too was faked. The scammers are experts in their field. You don't stand a chance if you get caught up in their web. It is avoiding the web and the pitfalls. It is learning how to identify the web and pitfalls.

However, it is not only about the scammer or being scammed as the reason I wrote this book. It is for all those people who want romance in their lives and some intrigue for whom I wrote this book.

We can wallow in self-pity of what someone did to us. That is easy to fall into, but it isn't what they did to us—it is what I did to myself as the reason I wrote this book. Since the scam is s going on as I write this, the ending will be a surprise to you, as well as to me. HOWEVER, there is a solution to this from which all you romantics can learn, as well as for the people who want intrigue in their lives.

Go out and live life. Don't go to the dating sites and take potluck. Find someone who loves romance as much as you do. Find the person who is as full of life as you are full of life, no matter what your age.

Scammers say age is relative, and guess what? They are right! By looking for Mr. or Mrs. Right, there will be some intrigue—there just will be. But scammers have the art of romance down to a "T", and they use other people's faces that make you want to drop your jaw in how beautiful they look. It truly seems too real to be true that someone who has money, looks, etc., is fascinated by you. Guess what? If it seems too good to be true...

But what I hope you will get from this book is to go out and use the money you are spending on the scammer to live your life yourself. Have a glass of wine on the beach by yourself. You never know who will come up to you and start a conversation—maybe Mr./Mrs. Right, maybe Mr./Mrs. Wrong, or maybe no one. But you will have a glass of wine on a beach and see a beautiful sunset. This is a given.

Take the vacation you always wanted to go on but never did. Go by yourself if no one else wants to go. Don't let things or people stop you. You only live life once.

I had forgotten why I was so happy when I was younger, and what I do owe to my scammer(s) is they made me remember me, the way I was when I was happy and alive. I thought age was the problem. It isn't age—it's complacency. It is sitting back and saying, "1'm too old." The worst part for me? The passion I felt was definitely real. The communication was definitely real. The love I felt for the scammer was so very real. They had me in a frame of mind that was truly euphoric— the best way I can describe the feeling. All the emotions and love I felt at the time of being scammed were spectacular, and no man in reality has ever given me that feeling thus far. It is very hard to explain to someone who has never experienced it. (However, it is not worth it in the end, so please—PLEASE— don't go there.) The part that was the worst part? They weren't/ aren't real. The illusion is there, but reality wasn't. That is my only regret: that it wasn't real.

The part that I am grateful for through all of this is I learned a whole lot. I learned a lot about me and who I am. I had forgotten me over the years. That may sound strange, but it is very true.

I learned a WHOLE lot about scammers and the many aspects of scamming. By the way, this story is only about my experience with scammers. There are many different realms and ways to scam. Some scamming is only done by one person; some scammers work in teams; some scammers work with your emotions; some scammers work with products; and some scammers, if not given what they want, have been known to threaten individuals from what I have read, and I am so glad not to have experienced that. Some scammers have scammed people in real estate, where people have almost lost their shirts (but this is a different story—for a different time). This story is a scam of the heart, which to me is the worst scam of all.

Hopefully, as you read my story, you will learn, maybe laugh a little, maybe cry a little, and definitely wonder, *What the HELL was she thinking...*

CHAPTER 1

START OF AN INCREDIBLE ADVENTURE

HMMMM... THINKING ABOUT HOW I should start this story which by the way is fact, not fiction.

I think every man and woman who wants true romance in their lives should read this and really practice it. We play songs of romance. We read books on romance. We fantasize about romance, but when we actually live our lives, we fall short—REALLY SHORT. Romance is an art to be practiced daily for every year and minute of our lives. For whatever reason, we don't do it. Some small minority do practice it daily and are the ones who are very happy in their relationships and stay married for a very long time.

Hopefully, this book will tell all of us how to get there and how to stay there.

I had it at one point in my life and was exceedingly happy but sadly lost the desire to keep it going. I must preface this by saying it is not just one partner who does this—BOTH have to engage and be fully committed in order for this to work. One partner cannot be the one with all the romance and the other just enjoy it without giving back in return. Plus, you must make your partner the most important person in your life above all others. Love dissipates when the partner believes they take a second seat to any other person. Trust me, it just does.

I am hoping, people who are younger than me will read this and actually practice it.

How did I realize this in such a late stage of my life? This is the interesting part.

SCAMMERS! YES—you read that right. Scammers—and of all places to find them, on Facebook. Not really where you expect to meet them, but they are there. Yes, I was scammed. I of all people, who is by nature suspicious and cautious, and I question everyone about everything, I was still scammed.

"Why?" was my question, and it took me a while to figure this out. I like romance—no, actually I love romance. I love the adventures in life. I am not talking about reading adventures but living adventures. Going places you have never been before, exploring the countryside, and actually meeting the real people of the country you are visiting and not doing the touristy thing but the nature thing and doing what the people do who reside there. Scammers are masters of romance. They know what to say and when to say it—well, at least the ones I met. Oh, yes, I did say ones I met. It wasn't just one but two but never actually met them face to face, and if you continue reading, you will find out why I never met them. When I say two scammers, I don't mean working together but two separate incidents.

It starts with a simple "hello" or "hi, "' and then you start talking about them and yourself. I tried chasing them away, but every time they came back with why I shouldn't. For example, the first one— let's call him John—was thirteen years my junior, and I told him he was way too young for me. I had dated someone ten years younger in my past, but that just didn't work out, and we met on a plane ride. However, he came back with a response that was along the lines of *"But that was then, and this is now. I am not a young man and am looking for someone I can relate to enjoy life with. Age is not that important as connecting to someone special."* Well, I found that hard to argue with because it is true: Age is indeed relative. He proceeded to tell me he lost his wife two years ago to cancer and had been living a life by himself with his son, who was twelve years old. He told me his son needed a mom as well. I was finding myself being attracted to him more and more as the days passed. He was dynamic, energetic, sensual, handsome, kind, and basically everything a woman would want in a man—everything! I kept thinking, *WOW how did this happen to me? This is the best thing since sliced bread...*

I should back this story up a little as well before I continue with the story of John.

I am kinda in a relationship with someone else. It started about twenty-six years ago, and it was perfect back then, but we never married. The romance was there. He surprised me with a single rose that he hid and later brought out later that evening. I, too, would surprise him with flowers at work or where he lived. We would take off and travel to Washington, D.C., just to have dinner and take a stroll and come back the same day/night. Sometimes we would just hop in the car and see where we'd end up. We didn't know each other for a long time before he moved in with me. When you love someone, you know quickly whether or not they are your soulmate. However, as we got older, the romance and the trips were less and less. Issues that came between us in our relationship were growing, and the issues seemed to sneak in between us. He had children (two, in fact—a boy and a girl). Yes, he was married but separated at that time when we first met. His wife was his soon to-be ex-wife, but somehow, she always managed to ruin our plans for travel.

I traveled every weekend, before I met my significant other, to someplace. The place never mattered to me; it was the experience that mattered.

My significant other was only introduced to the spur-of-the moment travel through me. He had obligations and I, too, took those on because I loved him with all my heart. I coped with his ex because I loved him very much. BUT (yes, there is a but) when talking to the scammer, John (I didn't know he was a scammer at this time), I realized that in all these twenty-six years of knowing my significant other, I had lost the fun-loving, crazy me. I wanted that person back. I am now sixty-two years old as I write this story, and longevity is not in my family. I may not make it to sixty-five years old (that is about the time my mom passed away, at the early age of sixty-four going on sixty-five, and WOW, I realized I'm almost there now). So, I was posed with the question to myself: Do I stay in the relationship that turned into a brother sister kind of relationship, or do what the old me would have done and go and spend the rest of my life in one romantic hoopla before it comes to an end? That decision wasn't hard for me. I was going for the gusto. I only have one life to live, and I am going out with a bang.

Let me preface this story before continuing on by giving you some of John's background information. He initially informed me he was single and a Catholic man. He had a son by his wife, whom he loved very much, but she had passed away. John's mother died when he was very young, and his father raised him by himself and never married a second time. John was born in Italy, but his father now resided in England and was quite old and feeble and in very poor health. John met his wife while in college when he was in England, and they moved to California after they both graduated. He told me he was 5'6" tall. He wore a size eleven ring. He loved to eat peppered roasted chicken, and it was his favorite dish. He drove a 4matic Mercedes Benz. And he lived in Los Angeles, California. His favorite color was red, and he loved red roses. He sent me pictures of himself and his son. His son was a sweet young boy, and John was indeed a handsome man.

His house was a very nice home, from the pictures I was given. He has/had a dog, and I was sent a picture of the dog, as well as another picture of him with the dog.

Nothing was unusual, and it appeared like he was the sweetest man and a loving father. He didn't look that much younger than me since he had gray hair. These were examples of the conversations we had prior to what would be occurring.

John's first conversation went along these lines, which I copied from Facebook before his Facebook account disappeared:

"Hello Beverly, good evening, first I want to thank you for accepting my request it was so nice of you, how are you, I hope your day was fine for you, I must say you are beautiful and you have got a great Profile, been friends with you is a Privilege. For starters, I am John, I live in LA, l am widowed, I lost my wife 2 years ago to cancer, tell me a little about you Pretty, are you single or in a relationship. I wait to read from you.

It was so nice reading from you, first I want to say I am a man who knows what he wants and when I find it I go for it, I want a woman with a different view of life, I want a relationship built on trust, true love and not material or things we see that's why I came here, meeting you has been a Privilege for me, I am into road, bridges construction, my job is etc..."

This one is after I informed John that what he saw was an old picture of me that was taken when I was his age, and this was his response:

Hello Beverly, how are, hope you are fine and you had a great day, it was good reading from you once again. For starters I will like to tell you everything you wish to know, I was married for 18yrs before I lost my wife, she was my first true love, we met during our college days, we dated for 2 years before getting married, when I lost her it was so hard for me to move on.

My likes, I love sports a lot, golf, I love swimming, I love to go out once in a while with my son and friends just to relax, I spend my evenings with my son, probably sitting outside getting some fresh air, on weekends, I take him to the park or cinema. I must admit life has been so lonely with a woman to call my own, I need a true mother for Micheal, a woman who knows what it takes to build a home.

I want to let you know I have never done online relationship before, when I met you it was different, even with the age difference between us, I still see you as a nice woman, a woman every man will like to have, though I might not have seen your recent photos, it still doesn't matter to me, because looks fade, but a sincere heart lives forever. Like I told you, I work as a construction engineer, I am into road, and bridge constructions, I have a nice income, I have my own home and my own car.

For my family, my dad is aged, he lives in London, I lost my mum when I was 5years old, had no brother, no sister, I grew up by myself my dad taught me a lot, to always love respect and treat my woman right, Beverly, I do believe there is a reason for us meeting each other, I want to grow with you, tell me about you, have a great evening.

So, after many conversations, he informed me that he was going on an assignment for fixing/repairing some lines in the Salton Sea, which is located in the U.S. This seemed normal, but after a few days at sea, he said his son dropped their phones in the Salton Sea when a major wave came and scared his son. John said he had to borrow someone's phone to talk to me, and he was having trouble getting access since the weather was bad. Since it was February 2014, this seemed normal. He asked if I could purchase phones for him since he was on the ship and had no way of leaving the ship. After I got mad that he needed two phones and not just one, he informed me that his son was with him and needed his own phone for schoolwork. This too seemed normal to me. So, I went out to purchase two phones for him because I was getting reimbursed when he got off the ship. However, he selected the most expensive phones on the market. I purchased the phones as requested but had to ship the phones to Nigeria—why, you ask? I asked the same thing, especially since I know cell phones are a commodity in Nigeria and they get top dollar for them. When I got mad and yelled and asked what he was pulling off because I told him I was aware of phones being worth a lot in Nigeria and asked him if he was scamming me, he informed me there was a colleague who was from Nigeria who had the expertise to work on the lines he needed. They were sending for him because of his expertise, and his colleague could bring the phones to him when he came since he was still on the ship with no way to disembark. This was still a reasonable story, and the person was at a university for the address that I shipped it to, and again it sounded reasonable. I sent it via a major company for sending packages at a cost of about two hundred dollars for express delivery. Needless to say, I am not a woman of means, but the more we talked, the more he stirred emotions in me that I thought were dead—and he did it with just his words and how he said them. This is very hard to explain unless you have experienced it. Because of everything I felt at the time, I sent the phones even though financially it was hard for me to do.

There was nothing fancy in what he said. He was not great in writing sentences or in sentence structure by any means. But remember, he was born in Italy, and he was raised only by his father, and he moved to England at the age of eighteen. So again, it didn't seem unusual that his English grammar was not the best. Mine isn't the best, and I only know English. But the words sounded like it came from the heart. The words and the meaning sounded like it was truly meant in all aspects. It was so deep that it actually got me sexually aroused without him even talking about anything sexual. He stirred feelings that I really thought because of my age were never going to come back. For that reason and other reasons, I had this strong desire to see him.

His picture on the internet was of this exceedingly handsome man. He sent me pictures of himself and his son that were taken on the beach and of him in his home, which was a very nice house, from the pictures taken. There was no reason to think this was not the real deal. Remember, he told me he lived in California and his wife died of cancer two years ago, and he hadn't really met anyone he liked or was interested in since her death. He wanted someone who was down to earth and did not feel the women from California were the down-to-earth kind. The women he met were more or less wanting the material things in life. He wanted someone who loved him and not the things/items he possessed. John told me my picture popped up on the internet when he connected with someone else. He was attracted to my picture and felt the need to connect with me.

This, too, was not unusual to me since I hear that a lot in my life. But remember, he was still on a ship, nice and safe.

Here are a couple of the emails I received when he was on the ship. In the first letter, he answered a few questions I asked him:

sweetie, you are so sweet, i don't smoke, i will call you when i wake, i love Pepper sauce and chicken, life with you is going to be great, i want you to remove the idea of an email ordered bride from your mind, people meet in different means, if God has made this our way of meeting then let's be grateful, i travel a lot due to my job, i have all i ever want in life, all i need is just a woman to call my own, a lip to kiss and a woman to call my own. i must say you are dynamic too, i thank God i found you, open your heart, feel like i live next street to you, that is the best way to develop love and i Promise you, you will be happy you did, from a distance i will make you happy, i will make you feel me so close to you, it doesn't matter how long we stay apart before we meet, what matters is how happy we live forever. Sweetie i will give you my all, my heart and everything, all i want is just your love and heart.

Baby i must say you are beginning to change my world, you are the sweetest woman i have ever met, wish i met you long ago before now, baby i miss you so much, no one can ever make me happy like you have done, as i read your messages i smiled, if i had one wish, i want to disappear to be with you, give you a sweet kiss and come back, baby now that you are mine i never want to loose you, i cherish you with all my life, no woman will ever come between us, as soon as i leave the sea i am coming to be with you. If love ever had a name, i will call it Beverly, of a million woman you are unique, i feel you so close to me, i close my eyes i see you walking close to me, i stretch out my arms and i reach for you, i miss you so much, i have never felt this way for anyone. I Promise never to lie, decieve or cheat on you, you are the best, if it takes my life to make you happy i will give it to you, the best life is all i want for us, i want to go on my knees before you, and put a ring on your middle finger, I thank God for bringing you my way, i •want to let you know the distance between us matters less to me for a know it will only be for a while and then we shall be together, i want to kiss your sweet lips, i want to make sweet love to you al/ night, i want to be the only one you think of i Promise to be the man who makes you smile, your comfort in distress and your warmth when you are cold, i want to be the man who wakes you up with a sweet tender kiss, my Plans for our future are so great baby, if i say i love you, will it get you angry or surprised, please don't be, because from the first day i set eves on your Profile i have loved and cherished you, i wish my arms were your Pillow as you sleep, i miss you so much baby, think of me like i always do to you, and I pray you love me like i have loved you, muahhhh

Just a side note: Again, having someone love me without seeing me is not unusual, plus I have had marriage proposals on a first date, so this was not that unusual, as you may think right now. So to me, this was not unusual.

Days later, he then informed me his son was getting ill, and I thought he just was seasick or maybe had the flu. I told him to wait few days and he should be better, but they had doctors on the ship, and he informed me his son had Wilm's tumor, had it for a while, and was awaiting an operation. He said his son needed three different kinds of medicines, and since he was waiting for the phones to be delivered from Nigeria, he asked if I could give the money to his friend in Nigeria so he could purchase the meds over there since they were less expensive. So naturally, I looked it up on the internet, and sure enough the meds he requested and the symptoms he told me his son had were that of Wilm's tumor. Here are the emails John sent to me in regards to the medicine:

Honey are you my earthly Angel, i bless the day I found you, and i Promise you there will never be a day when we will be apart, baby only you makes me happy and complete. You are the true definition of love, if love ever had a name i will call it Bev.

Baby the drugs needed are: Doxorubicin Hydrochloride, Dactinomycin, Vincristine Sulfate. Drugs cannot be sent to USA, the only means i can get the drugs is for the drugs to be bought by my colleague who will bring it to me when coming, baby soon i will be with you and i shall provide and carter for you and all your needs.

Michael had fruit salad for dinner as suggested by the medical team here to boast his hormones, i had just a glass of milk and some cereal biscuits, to be sincere, i don't feel hungry. Baby Please i want you to be sincere with me, "Am I putting too much stress on you", let me know, i Promise 1 won't get mad, for you i can never get angry because you are my joy, money matters less to me, because i have money, I can give you all you want and desire in life, all i want from you is just your love, if i had one option, i want to write your name up in the sky, so the whole world knows you are mine. muahhhhhhhhhhhhhhh

This may sound corny to people reading this. It sounded a little corny to me, too, to be perfectly honest, but it also sounded sincere.

Coming up with this money for the medicines, which he informed me was eight hundred dollars, was very hard to do since I am in real estate and I either need a closing or a rental in order to get paid. But wouldn't you know, the rental I was waiting months for was finally rented, and I magically had the money at the right time. So, I thought it must be meant to be. Everything seemed to be happening to accommodate his requests. Money now in hand, I went running to Western Union to ship the cash to John's colleague in Nigeria so that he could purchase the drugs from the university since he said it was cheaper there than the U.S. This too made sense because medicines outside the United States are normally cheaper than medicines sold in the United States.

Meanwhile, remember the phones? I was notified by the major mailing company that the phones were nowhere to be found. Where the phones were, no one knew at the time, not even the major mailing company, and that alone worried me. I kept calling the major mailing company and, after many phone calls later, found the phones got lost. Lost? And the major mailing company had no idea where they were, which was scary in itself. This to me was beginning to get comical in many aspects because the stories were getting a little ridiculous, but again, this was a major mailing company. I received a message from the major mailing company that the phones I sent via express delivery finally made it to their destination weeks after they were supposed to be delivered. The phones, I was told, went to a lot of places before arriving at the destination. I was so excited that the phones finally arrived at the destination, but they still were not delivered. No one at the major mailing company had a clue why the phones were not being delivered. I made several calls to management, as well as the upper echelon of the mailing company. Feeling a little frustrated (well, actually I felt major frustration), I sent John's friend (let's call him Kelvin) to the airport customs since that was where the major mailing company said the phones were, and still the major mailing company didn't know why the phones were never getting delivered to the person to whom I sent the phones. Kelvin then went to find out what happened to the phones. Kelvin informed me that the Nigeria customs department had a customs fee to release the phones. I wished the major mailing company would have informed me of all the fees before I sent the phones to Nigeria. Kelvin informed me he had no money to release the phones, and by this time it was getting past the hour to give Kelvin any money that he could retrieve before customs closed their doors for the day. Now remember, Kelvin has no money on him, so Kelvin said he needed money for dinner and a hotel for the night because now customs was closed. This probably was the only real part to this story. I did not feel like arguing with Kelvin as to why he could not go back home. So once again, I found myself going to Western Union to pay the custom fees and the hotel and meal for Kelvin. I must also preface this to inform you I did indeed talk to Kelvin, who was a very gracious and nice man to talk to/with. He was very polite and apologized for his lack of funds. Kelvin informed me that his lack of funds was because his wife had just given birth to their baby son. Once again, this seemed normal to me. The only abnormal thing to me thus far was the fact that the phones were having so much trouble being delivered. Kelvin, when he spoke to me, was, indeed, Nigerian from his accent.

Finally, after satisfying customs with all of their requirements, Kelvin finally had possession of the phones. Kelvin was finally ready to disembark with medicines and phones in hand.

Now remember, I was very worried about John's son's health and well-being and getting his sons meds to him quickly. However, I was still wondering why he was not life-flighted to the nearest hospital with his father. I worked at a hospital and knew if his son was seriously ill, the doctors would have life-flighted him to the nearest hospital. John informed me the doctors told him as long as his son received the needed medications, his son would be fine.

Kelvin finally arrived on the ship with the phones and the required medicines for John's son. All appeared to be going well for several days when I received an email that pirates (YES, I said PIRATES! Real pirates!) had arrived on the ship, but the security they had on the ship actually worked and the pirates left. John informed me that I shouldn't worry because everyone was okay, but the internet was messed up because security shut down everything. I felt so relieved that they were okay, and nothing happened. Of course, I looked up pirates on the internet, and sure enough, there are pirates who try to go on ships even now. So again, the stories I was getting were still checking out. I must also inform you that I am suspicious by nature and go to the internet for information.

I asked John to take pictures when he was on the ship and while he was working. John complied. He looked quite happy and content in the pictures.

Now as I am telling this story, you are probably wondering why John never paid for the meds or phones with money or credit cards. John had an explanation for this as well. The explanation was that he locked his bank accounts and didn't carry credit cards because they could be stolen or hacked, and after the pirates story, this too seemed feasible since there are still real pirates who are, to date, still out there on the open waters.

Please remember, we were still talking mainly through the email system, where he was still arousing me by just talking, but he had me where I felt like crawling out of my skin from the wanting of him. The sexual need for John was beyond belief. I wanted him so badly, more than I wanted any man in all of my sixty-two years of existence. The passion I felt was exceedingly intense. I felt he cared about me as I did him. To picture us in bed, making mad, passionate love with someone who totally understood me and I him, was most arousing to me. We connected on a very deep mental level—well, at least I did in retrospect. He was kind, considerate, knew what to say and when to say it. My ideal man was always the Marlboro Man—yes, the one on the cigarette cartons. It was a man who was good with his hands; handsome, but not a pretty boy; handy on all levels; and rugged. Plus, a man who knew what he wanted and went after what he wanted. That was my image of the Marlboro Man.

This is where the story starts to go a little awry. (I guess if you think about it, this whole story went awry from the get-go.) John then emailed me that Kelvin had gotten him a possible contract with the Nigerian government to do some road repair. The contractor before him never finished a job since he had some issues (the issues were never explained in detail to me). He said he wanted to write a proposal so he could get the contract. He asked if I had any problems with this, and I said no as long as I could see him before he left. He was due to leave the ship in about two weeks. This assignment was lasting longer due to the high waves and bad weather that they were experiencing when out on the open waters. He said we had plenty of time to see each other since the contract wasn't to start for some time. He did get the contract that he wanted, and he said it would be worth over five million upon completion. He even sent me a copy of the contract. We had many sensual conversations and how he wanted to take care of me and love me with all his might, and he asked if I would go with him to Nigeria when he went there to work. My first response was—Hell, yeah! I jumped on that bandwagon. I had envisioned touring with him when he had some free time and maybe watching him work and seeing what he actually did for a living. He said he could not be in Nigeria without me by his side. He said he couldn't wait to be off the ship so we could be together and all of the conversations we had—it had to be reality. However, my euphoria that I was feeling was now about to take a crash dive.

John informed me that he had ordered vats/containers of chemicals for the roadwork to be started for the Nigerian roadwork to commence. He received an email from customs that there was now a charge for the containers to be released from customs (as there was for the phones to be released). He had no money on him to pay this fee, and after the pirate story, I was now understanding why he would not carry any money or ID on him. I did ask him why he ordered the chemicals before he was off the ship or about to get off the ship, and his response was to have them ready, and it was never an issue before. I reminded him about the phone incident and asked why he thought it would be different for the chemicals. There was no response except he wasn't thinking and just wanted everything to be right for the assignment—and ready.

Several days have passed, and now he got an email and he informed me that customs were about to throw the chemicals in the ocean if he did not pay the fee for imports at the customs department. The fee was approximately twenty-one thousand dollars. I told him I couldn't help him because I didn't have that kind of money. He started to cry, saying he was ruined. John literally started crying. I know because he used Kelvin's phone to call me. The phones I gave him still weren't activated. He was in such a panic that he collapsed, and now his son called me in a panic, informing me his dad had collapsed and wasn't moving. I told him to get the doctors who were on the ship and to get them immediately.

Kelvin informed me later that John passed out because of all that he was going through and the pressures of the new assignment and now customs. Plus finishing the assignment, he was currently on. Plus, all the financial distress he was going through. Kelvin also informed me the doctors wanted John to rest and gave him sedation medication.

Before this all occurred, he did send me pictures of himself on the ship working, so I had no reason to believe he was not telling me the truth and was not the person he said he was. I still had my doubts and wrote to him about those doubts, but between John and his lawyer, they assured me the funds would be returned and that John was well off, and the money was not an issue with him.

These are the emails John sent to me in regards to him asking for the money to pay the custom fees:

Good morning my Angel, how are you, hope you are okay, hope you had a sweet sleep, baby I miss you so much, hope you didn't over panic, I am conscious now, Michael told me he spoke to you, he was happy, I am still very weak and still in bed, honey you know the reason I am breaking down.

Baby I got an email from the Custom and Working Commission, I have been charged for Licensing and Registration of the 2 containers, without this License and Registration Number I will not be able to clear my goods, the cost of registering the 2 container's is $960, which is $480Per container, baby Please help me with this first so my containerks can be registered so I don't lost them, baby please do this for me while we find a way to pay our Custom Charge and Tax, baby I hope this is not too much on you, I love you so much baby, muahhhhhhh

Good morning baby, how was your night, hope you slept well.

Baby since last night, I have had no rest, I am finished baby, I am about to get the biggest loss of my life, I got an email this morning from the Nigeria Commission On Works And Infrastructures and the Nigeria Sea/Custom Service, saying my 2 container loads of equipments and chemicals I bought for my contract has been seized and impounded, I wrote them asking why and they said the 2 containers were been held for Custom Charges and Tax, I have been charged 10% of my containers which amounted to $21,730, the 2 containers is worth $2,730,564, baby I have been given till 10th to pay up or get my containers confiscated, baby I am going crazy here, I need your help now more than ever, I lose this containers I have lost so much, I have no access to cash now, once I get off the sea I swear on my life I am Paying you back your money, baby please I need your help so badly, my heart is beating so fast,, I feel like giving up, the money is nothing to me but I have no access to cash now, baby please I need you to do this for our future, Pleaseeee baby, I love you so much, I feel so ashamed asking you but I have no one else now, honey Please do your best for me.

Honey I understand all you have said, I know it is not easy for you, I feel so ashamed and sad asking you for this, you have done so much for me, so much that Thank You will not be enough.

Baby my lawyer has no Say here, if I had a brother or a sister I would have gone to them, honey you know leaving the sea is not an option as I require Leave Permit to leave here which you know will not be possible as I am near contract completion, do you have an idea of how much I spent getting this contract and the equipment, like you know my account has been deactivated and so no wire can be done, baby you have done so much for me, I owe you a lot, but I am begging you, I need this contract so much, I am on the edge of losing over $2m to customs, do you think I will survive it if my containers get offloaded and thrown into the sea, baby I swear on my late mom, as soon as I come out together we are going to the bank and I will reimburse all your money back to you, baby Please, I need you more now than ever, I promise you this will be the last, I never should ask from you but I should be giving you, I feel so ashamed but I cannot let my containers go, if I could leave the sea believe me I will be off in a heartbeat, baby borrow from anyone, any financial institution, whatever be the interest rate I will pay, that money is little money to me, honey think about my health if I lose these containers, think about my future, I know you love me so much, honey please think of a way to help me raise the money, on my knees I am begging you, please do your hardest but never use your body because you are so precious to me, baby please I beg youuuuuuu, help me honey, pleaseeee

Just a side note: The reason why he mentioned never use your body" was because I wrote to John telling him the only way I could get that much money was if I sold my body and I doubted anyone would pay that much for a woman of my age.

John and John's attorney informed me there were penalties for not starting the work on time. In addition, John would have to pay for the containers themselves. The containers were ordered through someone John had an account with, but no payment was needed at the time; however, if the Nigerian customs were to throw the shipment in the ocean, he would have to pay for that shipment as well as another shipment. I still didn't send the money because I truly did not have it. The emotions were real—or so it seemed. The story, even though it sounded incredible, was still feasible. Plus, I was in love with John—so very much in love—but still, I gave him hell.

I then remembered I had a 401K that I am now of the age to get into, so I said I could give it to him but not by Western Union. He told me to give it to his attorney, located in California. I figured it was in California, and John's attorney requested I give it to his accountant, and she would then forward the money to where it needed to go. John's attorney informed me that he would handle all of the legalities.

HOWEVER, now John's attorney called me and asked if we could talk John into an assignment in Germany. It was less money, but it would probably be safer for him. Realizing how much trouble we had with the phones being delivered and the cost, I was concerned for John's safety. I was worried because the thought of John being thrown into jail for some really bizarre reason crossed my mind. So, I went along with the Germany assignment. John was happy and said he would talk to Kelvin about the assignment and how he would explain it to Kelvin so he would understand the fear level he too had. Because of the assignment change, John had to start the German assignment earlier than he would have started the Nigerian assignment. This was how he got out of the Nigerian assignment—by stating he forgot of an earlier assignment that he had to complete.

However (yes, another however), what John forgot to mention was he had to go to Germany directly after he left the ship. This devastated me because John had promised to see me after his ship assignment. I just gave this man over twenty-one thousand dollars for his life to be okay. I gave the money to John because I felt sorry for him, and I was promised that I would get it back when he went to Germany. I also felt a strong connection to him, a very strong connection. I cried for a couple of days because at that time, I was so sexually in need of him and felt like jumping his bones (literally). I wanted to grab him and hug him and never let him go. But he chose to go to Germany without a stopover to see me. However, to add insult to injury, he needed another five hundred dollars for Nigerian customs to release his containers in order for the containers to go to Germany.

Kelvin phoned me since he was concerned about John going to Germany and wanted to know if I heard anything from John and if he made it to Germany safely. Kelvin's sincerity in what he said to me made him sound like a very dear friend to John. Later that day, I did hear from John, and he had arrived safely in Germany. I then texted Kelvin that all was good.

Kelvin, as well as John's attorney, told me that John was a very sweet and gentle man and how I sounded the same way and that we would make a great couple.

However (yes, another however), when John went to Germany without coming to see me before he left to start his new assignment, I actually felt in my bones that I would never see John in my lifetime— ever—but I still loved him and was concerned about him.

I still loved John, but my love was not as strong as it was before, when he was on the ship. I felt abandoned in many respects but still cared and wanted him safe and sound—plus I wanted him to be happy. He was indeed a nice man and loved his son with all his might. However, I knew my love was waning. My Marlboro Man was not really my Marlboro Man. My Marlboro Man would never have such an emotional scene. My Marlboro Man would have held more of his emotions in and would have taken the blows.

Several days passed. The first few days, John was meeting with the workers, surveying the site, meeting with management, and signing the necessary contracts. John called and had trouble depositing his check in Germany from his last assignment in order to have the needed funds. I knew it would take approximately twenty days for the check to clear. He said it was different there but never explained what he meant. and I asked him to send me pictures of the area and of himself while he was away. He did this almost daily.

John took pictures of the food he ate and of the church he went to with his German translator whom he used while on the jobsite.

After several more days of being in Germany, wouldn't ya know, there was another issue. Of course. Why not?

He had the containers but needed the heavy equipment in order to do the work. Remember, he had no money because his check never cleared. This time John was requesting money for the machines he needed, and the cost was approximately thirty-five thousand dollars. John told me he was going to acquire forty-three thousand dollars for the first draw for the work he was doing in a few days after the work had been started, and he would pay me from that money. I went back to my retirement account and gave him the thirty-five thousand dollars. (This is painful just writing about this right now since it is still fresh in my mind.) But I gave it to him in the same manner as I gave him the twenty-one thousand dollars: via his lawyer, who had me send it to his accountant, but this time it was a different accountant. The first accountant wanted another job that was higher paying. His lawyer informed me that he had another accountant he used for clients who dealt with larger accounts, and we could use them. The people were in the United States, and we were using large banks in the United States to transfer the monies, so all should be good—right?

I asked John for pictures of himself and of his ID in order for him to prove who he was before I would give the thirty-five thousand dollars. He sent me his ID with him holding it.

The picture he gave is the following, along with his words, which he sent me in the email:

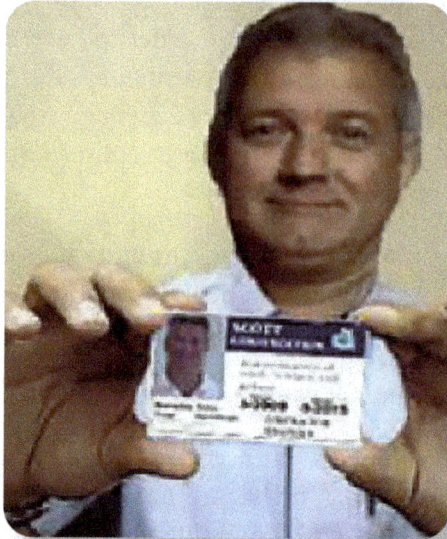

baby, i miss you so much. now i understand how much you felt
about me not sending you any of my credentials.
but anyway im here in the cyber cafe and taking a Pics of my
birth certificate and my working i.d.
i love you so much my world. Muuaahhhhhh

John also sent me the contract for this assignment. This contract was not as legal looking as the last contract. So, as I stated, I am a little suspicious of everything, and he complied with my request and sent me what I requested— PLUS he sent me his birth certificate, which I could barely read. John included a picture of his ID badge from the place for whom he was contracting, and the picture showed him holding the ID badge. He looked as he did on Facebook. A little bit worn out but the same.

A question that popped into my head was: Why didn't he go home and pick up some money before his departure to Germany? I did ask John, but he said he didn't anticipate any problems or issues with his check and the ability to cash it. He also stated that he had to depart in a hurry to start the assignment. I did wonder why I knew the issues with the check and cashing it and John didn't since this wasn't his first assignment overseas. Somehow, I dismissed my concern. Thinking back on it, I wonder why I dismissed it so readily.

Now please try to remember, when he went to Germany, so did his son. John told me he had corresponded with the school and received permission for his son to go to Germany with his father.

John pleaded with me for the thirty-five thousand dollars, and remember, he said I would get his check for forty-three thousand dollars minus five thousand when he got an advanced check that he bargained for when he received the assignment in Germany. He told me he would retain five thousand from the forty-three thousand for some expenses.

I had no reason not to believe him. He sent me pictures as I requested. He had reasons for everything that occurred. I kept looking at his picture and his face, pondering whether that was a face that would lie or tell the truth. His picture was that of an honest face. His son was a sweet boy. My heart went out to help him, and besides, I was getting the money back in a few days from his advance. Right?

This all seemed to make sense to me at the time, so I sent him the thirty-five thousand dollars. He made some friends with some of the people. The interpreter whom the company assigned to him for the worksite took him to church.

I felt better that he made some friends and was feeling better about being there. John sent me pictures of the machines that he rented and pictures of the site he was assigned.

No one really told me the exact spot because it was confidential. John sounded very happy that he was now working and had the much-needed machines in order to do his work—BUT several days into the work at the site and before he received his forty-three thousand dollars (money he was to send to me), he informed me there was an accident on the worksite.

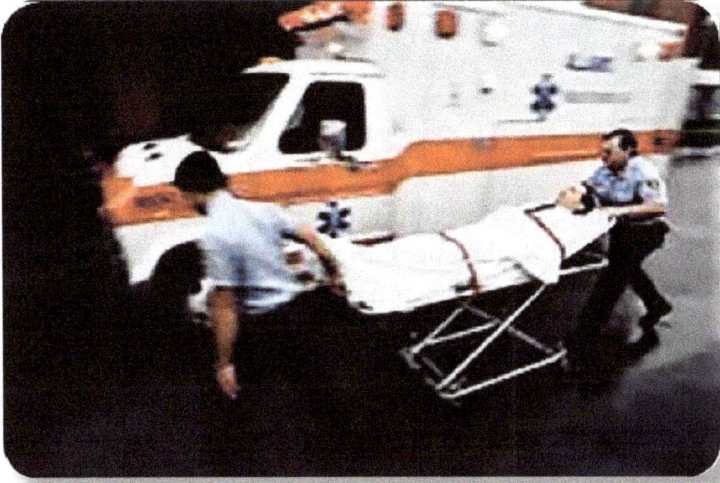

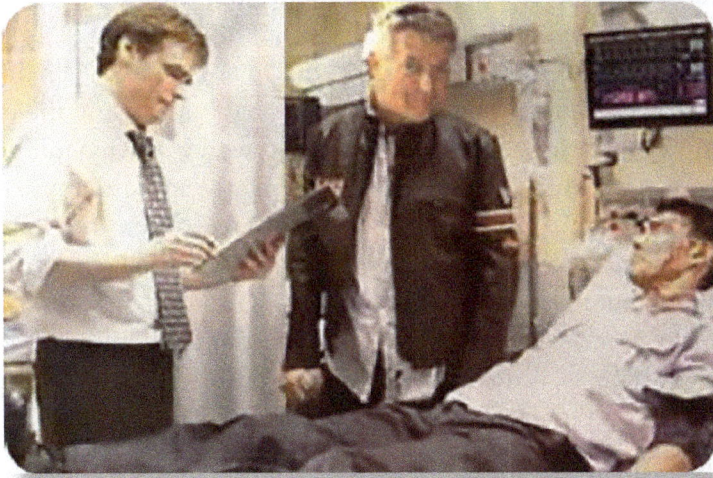

Why not? However, the accident happened with a Muslim worker. Please understand, it was important it being a Muslim worker (I will explain why in a minute). John called and said he was worried because one of his workers had an accident. He sent pictures of the overturned equipment, pictures of the ambulance carrying the injured man on a stretcher, and pictures of the injured man when he was in the hospital. The injured man in the hospital picture contained a heart monitor and the physician in attendance. All appeared normal in regards to the pictures and his accounts of the situation. John said the man's breathing was abnormal. I told him if his breathing was abnormal, someone would have placed him on oxygen, and the man from the pictures was not on any oxygen of any kind. John told me I was right and said he was going to his hotel room.

I asked John, because I was worried about his son, when he was at work and when he left his son to go to the hospital, then who was taking care of his son? John informed me he got someone to take care of him and teach him while he was at work. Again, this is normal for a father to do and to care for his son.

However (yes, another however), I received an email stating that he had to rush to the hospital and that he (John) received a call from the hospital stating the man took a turn for the worse. The doctor informed him upon arrival that the man had internal bleeding and the injured worker was in the operating room. John, while he was waiting for the doctors to say the condition of the injured worker, called me and sounded quite scared about the condition of the injured man. John informed me he sat in the hospital for several hours while the doctors were in the operating room with the injured worker. Many hours passed before John eventually informed me the man had passed away. John seemed in a panic, and I asked why. He stated when a Muslim dies at a worksite, his family will ask for restitution, and he was awaiting what that amount was going to be. I was unaware of this and naturally went to the internet to look up "Muslim customs and religious beliefs." Wouldn't ya know, it was there, in black and white. This too turned out to be true. I had no reason not to believe him.

We all waited for the family to inform their lawyer what they needed in order to be satisfied. The verdict was fifty-five thousand dollars. Lots of money. It took me by surprise, but I thought John took his check he received on the ship and deposited it, so I thought all was good. But guess what? I was wrong. He placed it somewhere else where he thought it was safe. Why would he do this? Because he was going to be getting bonus checks and advance money checks from the work he was doing in Germany.

Nothing seemed to be going right. NOTHING! I talked to John's attorney, and all I felt was worse. John's attorney informed me that the workers had to quit working because that, too, was Muslim law. Then I kept thinking, Muslim law? What the hey? What happened to a court trial? John, as well as his attorney, kept telling me that Muslim law had to be upheld. John went into hiding in a Catholic church (so I was told) since he was afraid of the Muslims and what they might do to him. He was concerned for his equipment at the site but could not do anything about the equipment.

John's lawyer informed me that he would refinance his truck and could get twenty thousand dollars for it if I could come up with the thirty-five thousand. I really had to think about this. How would I come up with another thirty-five thousand dollars? I remember thinking, was I totally mad for considering this? But guilt came over me. What if he really was going to get beaten or, worse, killed by the Muslims if he didn't pay the fee (as his lawyer feared) or end up in jail of some kind? I kept wondering what John's son was going to do without a father to defend or protect him in a strange country where he knew no one. John kept emailing me, telling me how much he loved me and how scared he was that he was going to die in Germany. I asked his attorney to write me a letter saying that if anything were to happen to John that he John's attorney) would pay full restitution to me for all the money I had given to John, as well as the phones and fees I paid along the way. The attorney complied. I was also worried this same kind of incident could happen again. I wanted some reassurance that this kind of incident could not occur again to another Muslim. John's attorney informed me that he came up with a plan to keep the Muslims away from the heavy equipment and told John to instruct the workers again on the operations of the machines they were assigned. After all of the reassurances, I gave the thirty-five thousand dollars. But guess what? When the time came to give all the money to the Muslims, his lawyer called, apologizing that he was unable to get his truck refinanced. He said John needed twenty thousand dollars for him to get free or otherwise there would be an uprising and most probably John would get killed in the uprising. Again, worried about John dying, I gave my savings to him. I would rather see a man live and be safe than to worry about my finances. I kept thinking of a small boy watching his father die a painful death. John said he was indeed thankful for all I had done for him and that he could go back and complete his assignment. John sounded so excited when he called and when he wrote emails to me and was really excited to start the work he was sent there to do. John informed me that he called the men together to clean off the machines and to start the work back up.

But then I got a call that the machines were not working, and another fifteen thousand dollars was needed for batteries that died in the interim and gas for the machines, so the last of the money I saved for retirement was all gone. But John sounded very happy and said he took his son to the site where he could watch him work. John said his son was so very proud of him when he was working. All seemed okay and all seemed good.

It was now Easter. John finished his assignment and, from the emails, was really excited to be done. Of course, he was done before he received any advance checks or bonus checks. He said the people he did the work for were really excited about the work he did. John informed me they were pleased due to the completion of the job, which was ahead of time even with all of the issues he encountered. John worked days and well into the evenings to get out of Germany as soon as he could. John was not happy being in Germany with all of the issues he encountered for the brief time he was there. John wrote to me daily, informing me of his day's activities.

John informed me they were having a party to celebrate Easter as well as the end of the assignment. The place, he said, ordered hookers/prostitutes to be there, as well as to satisfy the men's needs; however, he didn't go with them because he was only thinking about me and how soon we were going to be together.

By this time, I had no idea if I would ever see him. I had hopes that I would, but there was always a feeling that I would never see him in my lifetime. He was getting paid over two million for the job he just finished. The two million dollars given to John were funds to pay John, as well as the workers and for the equipment and containers.

Thoughts of John dying went through my mind. What if, when they ordered the helicopter to leave the site to go to the airport, the helicopter exploded and someone would tell me John and his son were killed. OR—would some of the Muslims still be upset with John for the death of the worker and take revenge? I did talk to John's attorney regarding my concerns, and he laughed. He informed me that Muslims don't go after objects, so the helicopter would be safe to go to the site and to take off safely. Plus he assured me that no Muslims would be around John during his departure.

Monday, the day after Easter, I was really feeling very happy now that all of the issues were behind us and John was scheduled to depart on Thursday, all he had to do now was to pay the workers their salary. I would finally meet John and his son. However, I still had thoughts that I was still not going to meet John. Plus, I had thoughts that if and when I did meet him, did I really want to be with him after all of this? I like to live a life of excitement and adventure, not of terrors like the terrors I had just been through. I worried day and night over John's safety, as well as his son's safety, all the time he was in Germany. I lost quite a bit of weight (losing weight was a good thing but not the way I lost the weight—with worry and panic). Later in the day on Monday, I received an email that he placed the money in the same account that he could only access in the United States but named me on the account as well. I was furious and asked him why he would do such a thing. I stated it was his money and not mine and that all I wanted was my money that I gave him back—that was my only request of him. (This is still painful for me to write since the saga is still going on, and I will explain as the story continues and the reasons why.) However, he said he did it that way because he felt it was safer than to have the money in the parish where he was staying. (He was still in the parish because he had no money and still was apprehensive of the situation and felt safe and secure there.) He told me I needed to get it out of the account for him to pay the workers the money they earned. I didn't want to download it to me, so I asked his lawyer to have the money go to his accountant and not into my account. He said that was okay, so I proceeded to download/ transfer the money from that account into the attorney's accountant's bank account.

I then sat down at the computer to download the money. I got one-third of the way through the download, and I got stopped and was now being asked for a cot code. I had no idea what a cot code was until I went on the internet to look it up. Some were negative, but it did explain a cot code. The cot code cost was fifty-six hundred dollars ("Cot code" stands for "cost of transfer"). Wow... After giving all I had, where would I get this? But I talked to the lawyer, who assured me it would be okay, and the money would be given back immediately once the transfer was complete. So, I gave the fifty-six hundred to his accountant so she could pay the cot code to the appropriate party. How did I pay it? From my checking account—yes, I did. I gave all my money to pay the cot code—EVERY SINGLE PENNY—because I was expecting it back that day. SURPRISE! I went to transfer the money again and got a little farther. I was so excited to see it progressing— BUT (always a but or however) I got stopped three quarters of the way through the transfer, why? There was now a tax code to be paid. I was so furious. When I asked the amount of the tax code, it was ninety-four thousand dollars. YES! Ninety-four thousand dollars! I emailed and texted the attorney—who was appalled, so he stated—and he said he was going to sue the bank. A few days later, he told me I had to pay the tax code for him to get the payroll money. This was impossible, for I didn't have it, and I told them I didn't have it and didn't expect to have it ever in my lifetime. The attorney said he could sell his truck for twenty thousand dollars, so all I would need was a mere seventy-five thousand. I told him it was impossible because I didn't have it and it was still way too high for me to ever attain. After many conversations, I asked if he could bargain it down or, better yet, that I go to Germany and barter on John's behalf. I thought if I went there, I could reason with them and also thought after all I had been through, John's attorney couldn't barter his way out of a paper sack. John and his attorney said it was unwise for me to do so. They informed me that Germany was still old school, where women were still not respected.

I then posed a resolution to John's attorney since I was talked out of going there myself. The resolution was that I take John's place in Germany so that John could go back to the United States and retrieve his money and then come back to pay the workers. If I were to take his place, then they would know he was serious and would be coming back, and if that wasn't enough of a guarantee, then John's son could also stay with me in Germany since they knew how much his son meant to him. This made total sense to me, but it didn't to John's attorney. John's attorney stated the company John did the work for did not want that at all. John's attorney said that their beef, so to speak, was not with me but with John. So, John went into hiding again. Not really sure if he was in hiding since it was the same place he had chosen for refuge as before.

Then I received an email from John. This time, in the email, John stated that in a written letter addressed to him, the workers who were never paid threatened to do bodily harm to his son. The workers said they wanted to be paid or there would be an uprising and that John's son would be injured. I asked to see that letter, but it was never given to me. Because of the threats John was receiving and all of the pressures from the workers and management, it was more than John could bear. A few days later, I received a text from John's attorney, telling me that John swallowed some substance in the attempt to take his life. This took me by total surprise. I knew by our talks that John was not a strong man, but I never expected him to take his own life. He was Catholic, had a son he adored and treasured, and talked about marrying me. I was so taken back, and then I realized John really didn't love me as he proclaimed. (Please understand, through this entire thing, even though you suspect that you were duped in a scam, it is very real in many aspects. You go through this whole thing like it is really occurring, where reality and fantasy are as one, and it is very hard to comprehend, especially by someone who has not been through this experience.) First and foremost was the fact that he went to Germany without even wanting to see me before he left the ship, and now he attempted to take his life when he knew that act would prevent him from ever seeing me. This was when the love affair for me was over, but still, I wanted to help him if this story was actually real.

The reason I believed it to be real was that the events that took place were so bizarre, who in the world would ever make up this story? If you were to make up the story, wouldn't the story be in the realm of reality? However, now I started to look at the bank screens. The bank was real. I had looked it up before I did the transfer of the funds. But now I called the bank. They said they didn't have a cot code and never had one. Plus, they sent me over to another department, where they told me the screen looked as though it was an overlay to their screen. I asked them if that was an issue for them, and apparently it wasn't. I sent an email to their fraud department and to date have never received a response. Plus, I then realized the email address of the person giving me the cot code was not the company email address but a regular email address that a common person would use. I informed the attorney of this, and he said the bank John used was a subsidiary of the company and it was located in Mexico. John's attorney informed me that he had talked to the bank as I requested. I requested John's attorney to pose to the bank that the bank only hold a certain amount and not the entire amount, which was over three million dollars. I thought if they held five hundred thousand, it would be enough, but he said they did not want to do that and it wasn't their policy. I asked exactly what a tax code was, and as John's attorney explained to me, the tax code was due because John owed taxes from when he placed the money into the account until the present and it amounted to ninety-four thousand dollars. I did ask who made the bank judge and jury. It was only taxes from the current year, so why was it late enough to hold three million dollars?

I was worried for so many reasons but mainly that this story was true, so I looked up Interpol on the internet and filed a complaint or a concern or whatever you may wish to call it. I was worried that if this story were true, a little boy was in jeopardy, and if it was false, this was the cruelest of all things that could happen to anyone. I was wavering between it being a true and factual story and that it could be a scam. But every time I talked to John or his attorney, they explained what was happening in such detail as though it was reality, but some things still didn't make sense to me. Plus, there were so many people involved with different addresses, different phone numbers, different email addresses, different everything.

Remember that I had all of the email addresses, as I stated previously, from all of the people who contacted me one way or the other, all of the pictures, all of the bank account numbers, and all of the emails, and I was sure they could look up all of the text messages. So, I decided to look for other complaint centers in order for them to investigate and let me know if this was true or false. I found IC3, which is a government site for online scams. So, I forwarded all the information I had to them so they could investigate whether or not this was true or false. To date, I have not heard a thing from anyone. I haven't heard from the bank in regards to fraud, nor from Interpol or IC3.

But my story continues. The attorney then said all they needed was forty-five thousand dollars and John would be free to leave.

Please note that this was a large drop in the requested amount. John's attorney said he would sell his truck for twenty thousand dollars, and all I needed to bring was twenty-five thousand. Again, this was another drop from what they originally told me they needed. But in reality, I had no way of getting the funds. The attorney informed me to refinance my home and that John would reimburse me when he was back in the United States. I knew I was unable to do this, so I decided to go along with it to buy time for some organization to call me back, but I had to prove I was applying for the refinance. I knew I could not qualify for a loan with what I do for a living, nor did I make enough to substantiate the loan process, but in order for me to prolong this in hopes that someone would get back to me, it was worth a shot.

Weeks had now passed, and all of the threats of John being assaulted by the workers had not happened. In addition, I had not heard from John for several days. I finally got a hold of John's attorney, and he then informed me that John's son had contracted typhoid fever. So, I looked it up, and sure enough, typhoid is still prevalent in Germany. This story was either really true because it was so absurd, or someone had an exceedingly good imagination. However, this time nothing was asked of me. Time was now going by, and the amount somehow went down to eleven thousand dollars, which I needed to bring to the table. I had to ask how it went from twenty-five thousand to eleven thousand, and his attorney stated he found someone who was willing to give fourteen thousand. "Who?" was a question that popped into my head, but again, I was never told who the mysterious contributor was who was willing to give fourteen thousand dollars for John's release. But I was only informed that someone was now willing to give fourteen thousand to assist John in his plight.

Oh, I forgot to tell you how we went from seventy-five thousand to forty-five thousand. It appeared that management was okay if John just paid management their wages in order to let John leave. Interesting...

HOWEVER, questions kept popping in my head regarding the workers who were going to riot. How was paying management going to stop the uprising for the common worker? How was management going to keep the workers away from John and his son? How was John going to safely leave the area without paying the workers, who were the ones threatening him and his son?

As I was writing this story, I got a text message from John's attorney, stating: "Hello Madam... There is very big trouble now. I hope this will not bring the both of us down. "

Now I was curious and asked what he was talking about, and I got nothing back except he would reply when he was done driving. The next day (YES, a whole day after this text message), I asked if he reached his destination from last night and if he was able to talk. John's attorney stated: "John was taken to prison yesterday." I then asked where John's son was, and I did not get a response.

John's attorney: "I will send you pics the police over there sent me yesterday. This is really getting out of hands."

Now my question was, who in the world was taking pictures of the arrest? Police don't. Not that I am aware of.

So, I thought this was rather good news in many aspects:

1. John wouldn't get killed, nor would he be severely beaten; and

2. His son wouldn't get killed in an uprising (I finally found out that his son was with the parish priest and in safe keeping.)

I informed the attorney that now he could talk to the court system and use reasoning to get John released. He informed me that he couldn't because John was guilty. I was appalled to hear an attorney, who was a longtime friend, confidant, and someone John named his boy after and who claimed to be John's personal advisor, thought his client was guilty. I said that he should be bartering for John to be released on his own recognizance so that he could go to the United States and have full access to his money and that this whole situation would be resolved once this happened. He, to date, disagrees.

As I write this book, this story is still going on, and I hope it will continue until one of the major law enforcements can either tell me this is a true story or a major scam that needs to be stopped. This is a very cruel scam because I have lost weight in worry. I will admit, I needed to lose weight but not this way—never this way. Plus, I have a very heavy heart because this story can sway either way. There are SO many people involved: three accountants, a lawyer, John, his son (I talked to a boy), and four United States banks (one was a major bank; the one he placed his money in is in the United States for online banking needs). The online banking system is mainly outside the United States, from what I gathered when I looked it up online. The online banks should be concerned that their name and screens were used in a scamming operation—If, indeed, it was used for scamming people. Plus, pictures of a man injured and of a physician (real or not, it doesn't matter; they're still involved in this story). If this is false, then it is a large syndicate. If it is true, this is horrible to go through something like this.

However, what happened in the ending part of this story is even more bizarre than the first story. Please continue to read on. It gets better.

IF the average man/woman said and meant what the scammers say, we would have many, many happy relationships. Plus, the spouses would be very content in their relationships and would not have to scan the internet looking for love. The scammer has the art of writing love letters and getting to your inner being, and that is so very phenomenal. Plus, they have the art of stealing love letters from the sites that write love letters. Scammers go to these websites and steal these letters and poems. The scammer alters some words, and you have romance. We write about love stories, we read love stories, but we never do the love stories. We fall short on action. We are ashamed what the other person may think of us. Plus, when we have that perfect man or woman in our hands and they are right there with us, we fall short in the romance department. I remember going to restaurants and sharing each other's meals—and what I mean by sharing is feeding the other person and doing it romantically. Scammers talk about doing this, and we want that and look forward to it, but when we have someone right in front of us, we don't do it. WHY? I did, but as time and issues passed, the feeling wasn't there anymore. BOTH parties have to follow through with the romance—BOTH parties, not just one. BOTH.

Scammers talk about all of the things they will do when they are with you, and your mind does the rest. For me, I was so romantically involved with John before he went to Germany and so sexually aroused, it was impossible to contain. He had me pretty much on his first "hello". Later, as time progressed, I didn't want money to be an issue when someone's/anyone's life was in danger. I am a woman who always professed money is not as important as people are, and I will remain that way until I die. I never want someone to be killed if I can help them. However, being scammed is another issue. The stories they tell can go either way. There is enough truth to make it real, and because John's story is/was so bizarre, I still worry that he may be in jeopardy, but how can I prove or disprove when I don't have the tracking abilities the government has?

CHAPTER 2

SCAMMER NUMBER TWO

SO LET'S GET BACK to John a little later in order to discuss my second scammer—yes, the second scammer on Facebook. This person was trying to say hello to me before John said hello to me. I ignored him, but he was persistent. In late May, I decided to answer him to find out why he was trying so hard to say hello to me. This was happening when all of the John issues were still active. I decided to answer to find out what he wanted, plus it was a diversion from all of the John issues. Let's call him Lance. Lance said I was someone who caught his attention when he befriended someone, and my face popped up on his Facebook site. I was someone he wanted to connect with. It was the same reason John connected with me. I read his Facebook page, and he had friends, where John did not. His Facebook page contained phrases that I related to on a personal/emotional level. Here are a few of his thoughts that he wrote on his page:

"You only live once, but if you work it right, once is enough."

"Life isn't about how many breaths you take but about the moments that take your breath away."

"There are only two ways to live your life. One is as though nothing is a miracle. The other is as though everything is a miracle."

"I'm selfish, impatient, and a little insecure. I make mistakes, I am out of control, and at times hard to handle. But if you can't handle me at my worst, then you sure as hell don't deserve me at my best."

"To live is the rarest thing in the world. Most people exist, that is all."

There were more quotes, and I related to every single one. I started talking to him on Facebook, and his English was not the best, but then again neither is mine. He said he was of German descent but was born in Ireland. He, too, was Catholic, and his wife died of cancer three years ago. He has a daughter who was twelve years old and whom he had with his late wife. His daughter, Deb, was currently attending a boarding school. He and his wife adopted a son, who was now twenty-five years of age. The son followed in his father's footsteps in his chosen profession. The chosen profession was a geologist. This was fascinating to me because growing up, I, too, thought about being a geologist and told him that. He said he wasn't that kind of geologist but a petroleum geologist. This somehow went over my head, so I asked what that was, and he said he found petroleum and sold the schematic codes of where petroleum was located to a bidder.

In talking to him, I found that he took my mind off of all of my problems. We talked as you would to any friend. He informed me he had no romantic interest and just wanted to be friends. Somehow in the midst of all that was going on in my life, I needed a friend and someone to confide in. It was easy talking to him and safe because he wasn't anywhere near me. Lance was living in England with his son. He was kind from his writings and fun to talk to. He said the same about me, and we seemed to click.

I told him everything in regards to my relationships, and as the days passed, I told him more and more. I told Lance about John, and Lance wanted to help with getting John free from Germany. He, too, didn't want me going to Germany by myself for fear that something would happen to me. He was caring, gentle, full of life, and funny (a great sense of humor), and I found myself falling for him. Yes, I did—one more time. He was also romantic. When he talked about his wife, it appeared he had the perfect relationship and the kind I always wanted. Remember, I had the perfect relationship but somehow lost it over the years, and slowly my relationship I had for twenty-six years slowly became the relationship I never wanted. It was a relationship where couples sit across the dinner table at a restaurant, staring into space and talking about the dogs rather than their day experiences. We still shared a meal but not by feeding each other but dividing the meals into respective plates. This is definitely not my idea of a perfect relationship— well, not the relationship I always wanted. The relationship that Lance told me he had experienced with his late wife was the kind I had envisioned.

Later, as we knew each other more and more, I asked what made his relationship with his late wife so special. Lance informed me she always wanted to try new things, she was his friend, and they made it a point never to go to bed mad at each other.

Lance told me he was 6' 1" tall, wore a size nine ring, lived in London, and had a master's degree. His favorite dish was spaghetti and the only thing he could cook. When he Facebooked me, he always used the stickers, which I thought were corny but slowly grew to love because it was a part of him.

Please remember that when John went to Germany, I was slowly falling out of love with him because he broke a promise, but that never stopped me from loving him and caring for him. When I say I loved John, by the way, I still do, but I am not in love with John. It doesn't matter if John is real or fake; my emotions weren't fake but real. Sad but true.

I was now starting to fall in love with Lance. Lance said it was a shame that I was in love with John, and I told him it wasn't so. I cared about John and wanted him and his son safe in the United States. He said he was glad and asked me if he had a chance, and I said he did. We talked about meeting in Vegas to see if we wanted to take this any further or just stay as friends. Vegas seemed like a fun place to meet to find out if there were any sparks. By now he began calling me and talking to me. Lance had an accent, but it wasn't an English accent and could have been an Irish accent, but I am not that good on identifying accents. His accent sounded like it had a touch of French flare. John, too, had an accent, but it sounded Italian with something else mixed in. But remember, John was born in Italy and Lance was born in Ireland. John told me he could speak fluent Italian, fluent French, and some Spanish. Lance only spoke English.

Lance was more articulate than John. John spoke several languages, and Lance spoke only one. So, this only seemed normal.

We were becoming very close, and again I found myself very much attracted to him. Lance was seven years my junior. Now instead of just going to Vegas for finding out if we wanted to be together, we were now talking about getting married in Vegas. How did that come about? I am still vague about that. A friend of mine brought it up, and I believe I mentioned what my friend said, and suddenly it was becoming true. I asked this same friend if she thought I was mad because I fell for two men on Facebook, and she said no and wanted to see me happy because she knew I wasn't happy in my current relationship.

Remembering Lance's first call to me, I was taken back and actually hung up on him. I had been receiving strange calls from out-of-country callers with many accents ever since John roamed his phone on his travels. I had no idea who was calling. I asked who it was, and the voice on the other end asked me to guess, at which time I replied with a smart answer to the effect of "Guess this!" and I hung up. Lance called back again after Facebook messaging that he would be calling me. His first words were "I knew you would hang up." So, he got his wish because I hung up again because I really wasn't in the mood for such games. I told him on his third try that it wasn't funny. I had been receiving strange calls that pretty much said the same things but with a different twist. I told him if he wanted to play games to find someone else. He apologized and stated that he wasn't aware of what I had been through. I realized after calming down that he was right, that he was unaware of everything I had recently gone through, and I was taking my anger out on the wrong person.

But now Lance would call periodically and was quite giddy when he talked, and I was finding myself looking forward to his calls. We talked almost the entire day/weeks on Facebook.

Lance informed me he hadn't been this happy for such a long time, and his son noticed his change in personality and was happy for his father and figured that his father found someone.

He informed his son and daughter about the Vegas vacation and wanted them there because he wanted them to attend the wedding. He did not inform his daughter of the wedding but was going to in time. He wanted to break it to his daughter differently because of her mother's passing.

A few days passed, and Lance informed me that he was working on some schematic codes, and he wanted to sell the codes to the California bidder even though he would get less money, but he wanted to see me and didn't want to wait any longer. Lance said that seeing me was more important than getting more money for the codes. He said he wanted to take some time off from work so we could be together before the Vegas vacation to explore the States together. This blew me away because he chose to go to California to sell the codes for lesser money. This was so romantic and sweet to me. This wasn't at all like John, who went for the money when all I wanted was for him to be by my side.

I was so elated that we were going to be together in a whirlwind of romance and just a mass of fun. He was everything I wanted. He was a strong man and a man who knew what he wanted and wanted to go out and grab the woman who made him feel like a man again. He was soft and gentle and never wanted to argue—he said it wasn't him. He sounded like my Marlboro Man—yes, the Marlboro Man showed his head again. Plus, he was so very handsome.

Now you may think this is strange that I could fall in love so quickly, but I, too, know what I want in life and from a man. When I first met the man, I spent twenty-six years with, I fell in love in just a few weeks, and we started living together. It doesn't take me long to find out if I have a connection or not. A man's core is either good or it isn't. Finding the core is sometimes a little difficult, and also the attraction both mentally and physically matters. I was not planning on making love in the dark my whole life. But I don't have that much of a life remaining. I am in my latter part of existence. By the way, the older you get doesn't make you smarter—it just makes you older. Plus, the hormones are still active. After this year, I don't think that lessens either—as we age, we push it into our memory banks. However, when activated again, life is what life is.

Lance said he had to get the schematic codes from Nigeria, and then I cringed. I asked him, why Nigeria? He said it was for his work and that was where he went. I told him I had no money to get him out of any trouble he might get into. He asked why I said that. And he also asked if it was because of John, and of course, my response was yes. He told me to stop it, and nothing was going to happen...

Well, needless to say, off he and his son went to Nigeria. He called me several times from Nigeria and was so happy that soon we were going to be together and how he couldn't wait for that to happen. Every day he talked to me on Facebook. I was so elated that I told my friends that I was leaving—I never said that with John. I truly believed it with Lance.

The last day in Nigeria, he texted me and said they were leaving for the airport and that it was raining torrentially. I slept with the phone by my side, awaiting his arrival in England and wanting to know if he was safe and sound. However, the next morning, the Facebook message was very long. He informed me that they were attacked on the way to the airport. He was hit on the leg and dragged and because his son refused to give up the briefcase with the computer and all the credit cards and money, they had on them. Lance informed me they hit his son on the head with a gun. I was devastated again. How could this happen? But again, it sounded feasible. They were in Nigeria. What more can I say?

Lance informed me the hospital needed to be paid. He wondered if I could give them seventeen hundred dollars for them to come home and asked if I could send it to a Nigerian who worked at the hospital and was kind to them. I said I could as long as I could get it back—yup, I did it one more time. Ya think I would have learned my lesson, but oh, no. So being the stupid one, one more time I went to Western Union, but surprise, this time Western Union refused to transfer the money to that person. Western Union actually turned me away. I could not send the money. Western Union asked several questions of me before they said no to me. One of the questions was: Did I ever meet the person I was sending the money to in Nigeria? Well, obviously, the answer was no.

I was now running late for an appointment, so I went running to the appointment and Facebooked Lance, telling him I was turned down and was unable to send the money as he requested. He informed me to go to another money transfer place, and I asked why when I was already turned down. Why would it be any different? Lance informed me to try it. He looked up many money transfer places and actually sent me the addresses and phone numbers of the money transfer places in the area where I was. I let him think I did try and transfer and allowed him to think that again I got stopped. I now had a bad feeling, so I told him it wasn't working, and I got a feeling that I was not supposed to do this. He asked if I could send five hundred dollars to someone the Nigerian knew in the U.S. so she could send it to him, at which time I did. I was curious if he was actually telling me the truth or lying to me.

A few days had now passed, and Lance informed me that the doctors were now telling him that his son was in need of an operation for an appendicitis and the doctors thought the blows he took in the fight triggered his son's condition.

Several more days passed. I got an out-of-state call, and for what I do for a living, it isn't unusual. HOWEVER, it was from the woman I sent the money to in the United States. Because I am on the internet, she was able to find my information and called me directly. She informed me that I was being scammed. Her lover was the same person and did the same line of work as Lance. She swore they were the same person because she talked to her lover for two years and knew his voice well. However, unlike me, she saw her lover because he was on web cam, and she proceeded to tell me how handsome her scammer was in her eyes. She showed me his picture. I was not that impressed with him. I listened as she told me more. I was becoming fascinated by her story. I told her he didn't look like the person I was conversing with from the pictures that I had seen of both. She told me her scammer had a son and a daughter as well, but they had different names and were different ages. She informed me that her guy was also a petroleum geologist who was Irish but lived in the United States but also had a London phone number and went to Nigeria for schematic codes. HMMMMMMM… interesting. Two men who had the same sort of background. It was unusual, to say the least. She informed me this was going on for a couple of years with her. YEARS! YES, YEARS! She knew him quite well, and they were going to be married. She proceeded to tell me how much he truly loved her and how her scammer swore he was not cheating on her with me. Now think about this for a minute. She had been talking to him for years and had never met him, BUT they were going to be married.

As she talked, I was getting more confused but intrigued as well. Why did she think her lover she never met was cheating on her with me? She swore he had an Irish accent. I couldn't tell. The backgrounds were indeed sort of the same and almost identical. Coincidence? But again, how many petroleum geologists have I met in my lifetime? None, and the only time I heard of this occupation was with Lance. Now I had a woman telling me her lover, whom she never met in a couple of years, had the same occupation as Lance did. Are you kidding me?

Now I had to find out what the hell was going on. So, I asked Lance. I informed him that I talked to the woman who transferred the money and who was swearing that he was her virtual lover and that she told me he was religious and could quote the Bible to a T. (She told me she was very religious, and I guess that was what her scammer preyed on for her.) Lance told me he believed in God but was not that religious. He asked why I believed a crazy woman. He asked that I go back to when we fell in love without the interference of others. I agreed. I am of the old-country way of thinking, where your business is your business and is private.

However, this was still bugging the hell out of me—it really was. The woman who called me called me again, but this time she wanted to tell me he wanted money again. He had asked her for nine hundred dollars. She told me she gave her pension money to him and had for several years. She told me she had no gas or heat or light (electricity) in her abode because she gave all her money to the scammer every month. She told me and her scammer that she was going to marry her childhood friend, who always wanted to marry her, IF her scammer was not going to marry her in a week. The worst part was she knew he was a scammer because she sent money to him from other women. She then would look them up and inform them they were scammed by her scammer. This story was getting worse and worse as she kept talking to me. She was now filtering money to her scammer in full knowledge of doing so. Then she called the women to tell them they were scammed so she would no longer have them as competition, and then she would keep in contact with them as friends. ARE YOU KIDDING ME? As she proceeded to continue to talk, she informed me that the other man she would marry, IF her scammer did not marry her, as her scammer promised, was a bounty hunter. Are you kidding me? If he truly was a bounty hunter, then why couldn't he find this person who was taking every single penny from the woman he loved?

She swore the two men were identical by a website called www.jdetector.com. If you place the email address there, it will pop up with their faces—IF they place it on their email website and let you know if they are logged on or not. What that tells you is nothing, really, but she wanted me to see their pictures because she swore, they were the same person.

She informed me of sites on how to find scammers, but I didn't have a pencil and asked her to email me since she knew everything about me now from the internet. She said she would but never did.

Boy... Right now, I had no idea what to think. Was she telling me the truth? Her story also had loopholes in it, and so did Lance's. Right now, my head was literally spinning. What do or should I believe?

If the woman no longer wanted to scam anyone, as she was professing, why did she send the first amount of money to her scammer/friend/pseudo lover and then after she sent it proceed to look up the women on the internet to inform them? Why not look them up before she picked up the money and then never pick up the money so the women would not lose any money? Obviously, she wanted her scammer to get the initial amount but felt guilty or jealous? (I am guessing here) if more money was being requested from the same victim.

I told Lance of the website www.jdetector.com and the pictures, and lo and behold, the next day the pictures were gone. What a surprise!

Now I was on a quest. What the hell was going on? So, I scanned the internet, and BOY, was I in for the shock of my life.

CHAPTER 3

WAKE-UP CALL

I FOUND GOOGLE IMAGES, where you type the name and their face appears. Interesting! So, I googled Lance and found a strange name of what appeared to be a website under the picture. SOOOOO I decided to click on it to see where the website would take me, and sure enough, there was Lance—and SURPRISE, there were thirty or so aliases attached to him with that of the same face but many different pictures of the same face and in many different circumstances. So, I started to type the names of all of the different aliases. Surprising what you find on the internet.

All of a sudden, I thought I found the right person who belonged to the face, and it wasn't Lance. He was indeed German, as Lance claimed he was, and I thought it would be okay to put his name in the book since he was the most abused man scammers used. Plus, I knew why he was the most abused man scammers used. He was gorgeous to me, and apparently a lot of women thought so, too, because they created a Facebook page just for him. His name is Uwe Hubertus. I would love to meet this man, but I doubt if I ever will. Some women have gone to meet him and said he was very gracious. These women were scammed from many countries. I have no idea if this man is married or single and found very little on the real man. But he is everything I ever wanted in a man. I found so many pictures of him, and he appears to be exactly what my fantasies were of him. But with my luck, the real man probably only speaks German and is married. The Facebook page states he is not on the dating sites and nor is he on Facebook. But ladies, he is gorgeous for his age, but again I have no idea what his real age is. Just writing about him is fun. But the scammer with whom I am conversing has the personality that actually matches the pictures. That of a fun-loving man. One who enjoys life and is not afraid to act out his feelings. What a man, my Marlboro Man but not. Geeze. Why was this happening to me? I finally found the man I fell in love with, and he is totally fake. BUMMER!

So, of course, I confronted my scammer, but he said he was the real deal, and I would know he was when he held and caressed me. I asked questions of him to find out what the answers might be. I asked him what kind of clothes he likes to wear, and he said it depended on the occasion, then I asked if he liked to wear subdued colors or bright colors. Lance said bright colors, and so does the original from the pictures online, but if I know this so would the scammer.

You know, of all things, I have to admit when I talked to Lance, he actually seemed real and at times not so real... When I got quotes like:

"When I talk to you, it seems all the problems in the world go away and I'm floating in midair. Only God's creations can compare to the beauty that I see in you. My love for you is infinite, without limits."

It actually made me want to melt, and apparently many other women felt the same way. I copied that directly as written to me on Facebook.

This started me thinking about John. This was when I read those scammers create videos and talk via the internet, so you are seeing the person they copied. The pictures like the ones I was sent in emails can be faked. This is not just a one-person effort but much larger.

We allow this to go on because we don't have enough people to actually care about it? With social media, this will increase, and the crimes will be getting more and more serious. It stated on the internet that some of the victims actually get threatened if they do not give the money. So, people are living in fear? By not giving money? This is so wrong. My scammers were not like this, and I not only had two scammers—I had many phone calls because John roamed his phone. I did not hear John's voice a lot because he seldom called me because he always had phone issues, so it was hard to determine his voice when I received these calls. Some calls were erotic in nature, and I knew it wasn't him. John had a very romantic voice.

As I am writing this story, I have just (right now) found out that John has been jailed.

Both of the scams are going on as I write this book. Why, you ask? Because in some respects, I want them caught so this will never happen to someone else.

If I keep them wondering what I am doing, I am hoping the agencies I notified have enough time to actually catch them, but right now this seems very unlikely. I haven't heard anything from any agency.

Remember earlier I was informed that John was jailed, and I kept asking John's attorney to send me the pictures he claimed he had of the arrest. Well, today the lawyer sent me the picture of John being taken to the jail.

It is now I finally woke up and realized all that worry and sleepless nights I had were all in vain while they laughed their way to the bank with the money I handed over to them. How did I finally come to that realization?

The picture of the man jailed was faked and noticeably so. The face was placed over a much thinner body. Please note that this man has

no neck. This is the worse picture ever doctored to prove a point. I know when I ask the attorney why John is so thin, the answer will be that he hasn't eaten for months. But even the hands are different and appear to be of a younger, thinner man being jailed. Plus, John also has a thin smile on his face. Why, if you were being jailed, would you be smiling? Plus, he is wearing a heavier coat, and it is summer in Germany, so why would you be wearing a heavy coat?

I am including the pictures of the poor men who are being abused. The faces you see are not of the scammers. The scammers go hidden behind the faces of these poor abused men. Both are very handsome men who would catch any woman's attention. BUT you may ask, why am I showing faces of innocent men who were not part of the scamming operation? Because if you see these faces, please be aware these may not be the men you are dealing with at all. IF you see these faces on the internet, go to http://images. google.com/ and check the images of these men. When you go to this site, please enter the name of the person you are dealing with in the space provided, and all of the places (websites) they can be found will pop up along with all of the images of them. Hopefully you don't get totally shocked like I did when I looked up my second scammer and found the same pictures with thirty or so names attached to them. A definite WOW moment for me—it really was…

CHAPTER 4

HARD REALIZATION

NOW I DECIDED TO go back to the other pictures t •a Fent to me by John and to look at them closer than when I initially did. Now I was looking at the pictures in a different light because of what I found out on the internet to what scammers actually did to Uwe Hubertus's pictures. The pictures I was given were indeed doctored. They even used a picture of an injured man. How cruel can you get in order to get the sympathy you needed to acquire money? I can now see the doctoring of the pictures when I could not before. Why? Because with all of the loves in your life, you see through rose-colored glasses. You believe them. No one can be this cruel to make up horrendous stories of a boy being threatened and a man going in hiding in fear of his life.

John was not a face on the website I gave you, and the scammers you come across may not be. I really thought the story of John may have been real since the tale was too bizarre with medicines being mentioned and the condition of a small boy, which is not common. In addition, many people were involved and are/were located in the United States. Plus, the Nigerian addresses that the phones were to be delivered to were real.

I keep going through my mind of why I responded to John initially, and all I can come up with is it was the time of my life that I wanted something different than what I had. The picture of him was that of a very handsome man and a face that was an honest face and a sincere face. The picture of him and his son together was that of pure love. It never occurred to me that people were hiding behind pictures of other people. Plus, talking to John, he stirred emotions I thought were dead. I, all of a sudden, realized the me that I liked, I actually lost over time. I was in the shadow of someone else. SO, if any good came out of this, it was the fact that I am back in full fury and my ending years will be a blast. Why will my ending years be a blast? Because I am going to make them one. We are all in charge of our own destinies. What we do and how we do it is really up to us.

However, I am a little poorer right now but not for long. I will owe the government large amount of taxes and will be broke for a few years to come on money I never used myself, but so goes life. I really believed I was truly helping a person in need, and I hope I never lose that part of me, either. However, I will be a little smarter. The money I give will only be to the people I have met or organizations that are established.

But people also blame the scammer when we are at fault as well. We are all looking for romance, but how many people actually practice it? Few do, and they are the happy people with long, healthy marriages where both parties to the marriage work at it daily. Lance was right when he said to never go to bed mad at each other and to try new things and to be friends with each other. Have the dinners together and talk about the day you had. The things that Lance actually said and seemed to care about, like breaking the news to his daughter slowly so she would feel comfortable and at ease with the news of us getting married. This seemed so real to me because a caring parent would break the news of that magnitude to a young girl in that manner.

SO how does one tell a scammer from the real deal? I guess the only thing to do is what Lance said to do: See the person in person and hug and caress them. This is the only way to know if you are being scammed. Do not send money unless you really want to send money. Ensure you are sure who they are, and since I found out about videos and pictures being faked as well as PASSPORTS— how are you to be sure? The only way is in person. This is the only way. Poor Uwe has passports with other people's names on them with his face. I would love to meet Uwe in my lifetime just to say hi, whether he understood me or not.

The interesting part to this is I informed Lance that I was going to go to Nigeria to personally give him the tickets so he could go back to London and that I could stay with his son to keep his son company and keep his son safe while he went to London to retrieve the money he needed to pay the hospital. The end result was precious. Lance, all of a sudden, gave a response that caused me to be surprised. I really thought his response would have been that it was too violent in Nigeria and was not safe for a woman to go on her own and to carry a large sum of money, which would make her an easy target for thieves. BUT instead, the response I received was: "You are treating me like a child. You don't trust that I can purchase the tickets on my own without you being there. If you must see me, then book a flight to London, where we can meet and not in Nigeria. I will not be treated like a child."

Now I was even more ticked off than I was before. I told him the response, if he truly loved me, was: "I know, I really want to see you and be with you as well. I am so tired of being locked up in the hospital, and it is becoming a prison to me. Please come whenever you can and are able to come. I will be waiting to see you, but please be careful in Nigeria since there are some unscrupulous people here, and be sure that if you are carrying money not to let anyone know the amount or where it is hidden."

I told him the response he gave was dumb and not at all reasonable or understandable. We quit talking for a day or so. I know he is a scammer. There is no doubt in my mind right now. I decided to play a game with both of them. If they can lie their asses off, then so can I. Fair is fair.

As for John, I am 100 percent sure he is fake and now rich from the money I gave him. The arrest picture cinched it for me. That is so fake, it is ridiculous, and you can see for yourself. The head was just planted on another person's body.

CHAPTER 5

TRYING TO SCAM A SCAMMER

TODAY I TRIED TO scam the scammer. I asked John's lawyer to give me his five thousand dollars that he had remaining from the twenty thousand he said he originally had. I told him I needed the five thousand in order to get the loan. I told him I could get the entire amount needed, but I needed closing costs since I originally told them I could try and refinance my rental property when they said they needed more money. I told the lawyer it was a little more than the five thousand, but I could probably get the rest. He told me that John was my man and only thought I was asking him about the five thousand to put it toward the money needed. I told him no, that I needed it to get John freed, and the only way to get the money to get John freed was to get this loan, but I needed the five thousand he had in order to do this. He then said no, he couldn't send it. So, I decided to inform him that he would rather keep his five thousand than to give it to me and allow John, his best friend, his employer, his confidant, his friend of over eighteen years, to live. I informed him that if he did not give the money, which was our only hope for John to live, he would be condemning his friend to a jail term. I have not received my answer—yet. I am sure I will.

Amazing, because several days later (July 23, 2014), after asking John's lawyer for the five thousand dollars, John wrote to me (emails) from prison? Yes, from prison. And this was what he stated:

Honey it been so tough for us here, even in this hardship I think of just one thing, and that thing is you, i miss you so much, it's been months of you trying to get a loan to get me out, but i still never heard anything Positive, honey please do your hardest for me, i wanna leave here, I have been so sick for the past 4 days, life has been so unbearable for me, honey remember all our dreams together, i am counting so much on you, you have done so well for me but please get me out of here, at least to save Michael, as a boy he has suffered enough, honey pray for me also, i miss your sweet kisses from your honey lips, how is your health, please be strong for me and never give up on me because i can never leave without you, honey save me and Michael out of this hell, i love you and i pray i get a positive message from you, mwahhhhhhh

Now remember, I never met John, so how did he miss sweet kisses from my honey lips? Just curious of how that happened.

This was my reply to his email, and remember, I needed to keep his interest. So please bear that in mind when reading this:

John, Me Love,

I told Richmond if he was able to give me the 5K he claims he has than I could get you out because I need a little more than the 5K for closing costs but he won't part with it to get you out of jail... and back home. Your issue right now lies with Richmond... I found a place to give me the loan but giving the money for the cot code left me cash poor... so I have no money for closing costs... I have been in a hole trying to dig myself out ever since the cot code. So again, talk to Richmond. He said it was my issue and not his. Since he got you into this assignment/mess I think he needs to give something towards all the money issues. What he did with 15K is beyond me... He has the 5K... if he spent it after l told him then he is the one you would have issues with... I have to earn enough for closing costs to get the loan... I worry about you and Micheal daily..

Where are you both? Are you in jail and if so which one? and where is Michael. He must be terrified Without his Dad... Tell me where he is so maybe I can get him.

I have a question... How do you have access to a pc in jail? Do they allow you PC time?

I am so sorry you are sick... What is wrong with your health? Just feeling down or do you have a fever?

Hon I wish I wasn't cash poor but I am... only Richmond has enough to get me the loan... I have to pay closing costs to refi a home and I don't have the monies—I gave you every single penny I had... Richmond knows this and I have no idea why he won't give it. and he will probably tell me he spent it like he always does... If you want to be out soon—talk to Richmond...I already told him this and he got rude and said it was only up to me...I thought he was your friend... if he truly was/is your friend he would give it without batting an eye... or he would attempt to help me but he isn't... he just isn't...

Still love you... Hope you know that and never forget it... try and stay healthyfor me ok?

xxxxxxxxxxxxxxxoooooooooooooooooo

Please remember, I was not trying to get a loan. Now that I know this, too, was a scam. I had no intentions of getting a loan. I was trying to scam a scammer even though there was a slim-to-nothing chance of this working. However, if they were greedy? It might work if the greed outweighed money of 5K. If I did receive the five thousand dollars, then I think that would make me feel slightly better. But it's hard to scam a scammer. They have it down to a fine art. Yes, they do.

Several emails later, John was worried about my health. I was delaying him by telling him I was sick. My email to John:

Hi My Love...

I guess my health took a turn when Richmond refused to give the money he had to help me get the loan. My nerves just really got to me with you being in jail and not knowing anything about Micheal and Richmond being such a prick...

I gave everything I had to help with the cot code and it left me in such a big debt hole... I can get the loan but I need money in order to close. I needed Richmond to give me the 5K he said he had. If he gave me the 5K... actually 6K would be best... I could get the entire amount and you can be finally freed.

Without Richmond helping it is going to take me a little bit of time to get the money in order for closing to occur. He was so rude and didn't care. I told him I could finally free you and give the entire amount but he won't do it... Haven't talked to him since that time... then I became really sick. They informed me it was nerves... taking this time off from work hasn't helped me either since I had a hard time working...

See if you can talk to him... Love YOU!... Tell me how you and Michael are as well'... thanks Hon!

His reply to me:

I spoke to Richmond too, he has been through some troubles, his wife had an accident which left her Paralyzed, he has spent so much on her health this is why he wasn't able to help again, honey forget about getting the money from Richmond because he is in trouble, please look for another means to get the money, yesterday Michael was so hot, i cried all night, i lost my ex-wife, lost my mother, now my only son lies so sick, i hardly eat, to make matters worst I am in prison, you are sick, if i have any hope of leaving here and saving my only son this hope lies with you, my love please do your best for me, do not get angry, if I or Richmond have said or done anything wrong to you please forgive us, think about our future we will build together and save me, please pray for me and Michael, you are our only hope, I hope to read from you when next i have access online, i love you

This was so absurd. The lawyer's wife had an accident that left her paralyzed? REALLY? Now his son was also ill with a fever? John was in jail? Knowing I, too, was sick (so he was made to believe), I was the only one to save them? REALLY? I replied:

So so sorry to hear... but if Richmond gave me the money to close, I would be able to give him the money back... or you can give him the money back. Please ask him so he can give it to me and them everyone will be ok. ok?

Love you...

John's response back to me:

My love, After the treatment of his wife, Richmond is left with nothing, it hurts him i am still here but he has no cash now please do your hardest for me, i do not want to lose Micheal, take good care of your health for me, please i hope to hear something sweet, i love you so much, my heart beats so fast for your next message, muah muah

Obviously, scamming a scammer was not working out too well—and John's son, Michael, went from sick to dying. AMAZING!

To make matters even worse, John was now threatening to kill himself if I did not write to him. Remember, I told him I was sick, but from his writings I had to communicate with him often, which meant there was no concern for my health and wellbeing. He might say there was concern for my physical and mental wellbeing, as he does below, but it had been less than one week since I responded to his email. Below is his email to me:

Honey are you okay, how is your health, i might be in prison but you are always in my heart, i have not heard from you in a while and this makes me so worried, please write me so I know you are okay or i will kill myself love you so much, muahhhhhhh

Remember, he tried to take his life before. They will go to any length to have you save them. This is a little drastic. However, these are the types of emails you will get. REMEMBER, -THIS IS IMPORTANT- **IT IS FAKE!!!!**

As for Lance? One hell of a smart scammer. Lance is exceedingly intelligent and knows what to say and when to say it. He doesn't pressure you for money, either.

Where is Lance to date? He is still in the hospital with his son. How long have Lance and his son been in the hospital? To date it has been one month. The hospital is allowing them to stay in the hospital until the hospital bill is paid in full. Lance is allowed to leave, but his son cannot.

Lance claims they will allow only one to leave knowing the one who leaves will come back for the other. However, to leave the hospital and to go to London to retrieve money in order to pay the hospital bill, Lance needs a plane ticket. The ticket cost? It is roughly two thousand dollars, plus you need taxi fare to go to the airport. Lance claims he has asked a couple of friends, but they are all self-employed and have gone through some rough times. So, who does that leave to purchase the plane ticket? Yes, you guessed it. Lance knows the story of John and that I am having a rough year financially, but does that stop him from asking? NO, of course not.

Now remember, he was going to the airport when he got attacked. The plane tickets were confiscated with everything else. However, the airlines said they would honor the tickets. However (yes, there is a however—always is with scammers), Lance bought the plane tickets together, and it appears that one person cannot board without the other person boarding? Lance claims it isn't the airlines so much but the Nigerian customs preventing him from boarding. The customs department needs a doctor to write a letter as to why his son cannot board (his son cannot write this letter). HOWEVER (yes, still another one—always a however), the doctor cannot write this letter without the hospital bill being paid. Lance did try to bribe the doctor and nurse to write one, and he informed me he was taken to prison, where he explained what occurred to the police officers. The police released him back to the hospital, where the hospital administrators raised the hospital rate on him for doing that stunt. The doctor was placed on probation, and the secretary was fired. Therefore, he and his son are still in the hospital until he can raise the money for the plane ticket and taxi fare so he can fly solo in order to get the money from his account to pay the hospital bill so he and his son can go back to London.

This is the email I received in regards to him trying to bribe the doctor:

Yesterday was horrible after bribing doctor and secretary with the money you sent I had my few stuffs packed and was ready to leave... I had already said good bye to Andrew and that I will be back never knew I was being watched just as I stopped the taxi to leave I was stopped and asked where I was going and I explained that I have was leaving to return and I confidently said I had sorted things out with Doctor that I was leaving to go get money and be back to clear hospital bills so we can leave... they saw note from doctor on me and the questioned I how I got note I explained that doctor have me note so I can fly and go get money to clear bills. that's was the beginning of it all I was taken in and to the doctor who signed note to explain why I was giving a note without paying the hospital bills... he and secretary couldn't say a word before I knew it they called in Polices and the doctor and secretary where arrested and I was taken to police custody to give my own side of the story they kept me there till this morning... the doctor and secretary that took bribe are held and in police cell secretary was sacked at that very moment for taking bribing and going against hospital rules... doctor placed on probation... I do not expect anything from you cos I know you had tried your very best this I my fault and I take the blame for all that's happened... I don't want you worrying about us please like I will wait till am able to come up with flight ticket so I can leave to go get money and be back for Andrew but as it stands I can't and I can't have you worry about us...you mean note than you can ever imagine to me and I can't have you do something that would hurt you cos losing you would destroy and I don't think I can ever in this life recover from losing you... I understand you wouldn't want to talk to me anymore I certainly do cos this has been hell of both of us just know I love you now and forever and if you don't want to keep in touch that's okay I will contact you as soon as we able to get to London GPS you are my heart beat and my missing ribs and there's nothing I would do without you in my life...

With tears pouring from my eyes I write this

LOVE YOU NOWAND A DAY LANCE...

I did mention to Lance—in fact, today—just to see what he would say when I confronted him with pictures of himself that look exactly like Uwe Hubertus (one more time). His response? "I have a lot on my mind right now with trying to go home. I don't want to worry more in regards to this issue. Why are you bringing this up again? I told you when I hold you, you will know then who I really am."

I then asked Lance, "What happens if I never see you?" He said to me, "What makes you think I will never see you?" There is nothing he says that states that he is not the real McCoy.

The jury was out on this one (not really) until yesterday, when he knew every word I said about my sales and closings. He knew it down to a "T". People will remember some things said but not all, but for my sales and closings, he was asking about them. I made them up for a test. I didn't have them. I figured if they can do it, so can I. I wanted to find out what is important and what isn't. Apparently, the money is important. The question I have is: Why is there only money to resolve these issues? I know I can talk my way out of a lot of situations, especially since my words are real. Another question I have is: Why am I the only one who can assist? I know if I had a twelve-year-old daughter and she knew I was in trouble with her brother, she would talk to teachers, counselors, and friends about the situation. Someone would think of assisting or fundraising. Yet Lance never said she was doing anything in regards to this. This just seems natural to me for a daughter to do something, especially to talk to someone if she knew her father and brother were stuck in another country.

I will continue to postpone in hopes that the organizations who are to control the internet scammers kick in. Today, Lance said he missed me and our conversations. This sounded real and that he really meant it. Lance tells me to drive safely, to take care of myself, and not to work too hard. His exact words in just one of the messages were:

You just drive safely and know you are always in my heart and thoughts.

In many aspects, it is real since they are real people, just not who you think they are. He asked how I was feeling and how my day went, but I know the underlying concern is: Did I make a sale today? Might I say Lance is a good scammer. His English is so much better than John's, and his concern for my health and wellbeing does sound legit.

Lance's latest to me was this:

Our ships are moored in opposite seas; destiny brought us together but keeps us apart. We just can't be—you and me. There are a million miles between us. Obligations hold us at bay. We search in the dark for each other, but so many boundaries block the way. Yet I love you no less than if you were here. And I promise that my affection will not grow weary. 171 take you with me al/ of my days, with all the love a heart can carry. And I'll hope with a smile and heavy tears that the same thing that keeps us apart, will bring us together soon I have faith that someday we'll be— you and me. love you always...

This to me sounded like he was telling me goodbye for a while, but instead he informed me he was declaring his love and that his love would never die.

And this one, too, was recently sent to me:

There's so much I want to say to you, but no words seem strong enough express the depth of what I feel for you. I can only say that all of my life Eve looked for someone like you. I wanted to share my life with someone who's kind, affectionate, intelligent, Passionate, responsible, caring, easy-going, considerate, generous, determined, and hardworking. I've dreamed of someone who loves animals, children, romantic strolls beneath the moonlight, and long lazy nights before the fire. I wanted someone who has a good heart and cares about others, someone who's willing to go that extra mile for someone who's in need. You're all of these things and so much more, and Tm overjoyed that you're part of my life. And though I care about you more than words could ever say, 17/ say it anyway... 1 love you with all of my heart and to the very depth of my soul.

This one takes my breath way. It was a "WOW! HOLY COW!" moment.

Even though I know it was someone else's words he found from the internet, then again so are cards we purchase and give to friends and loved ones.

Lance I will miss—quite a bit. I have fallen very deeply in love with him even though I know he is not who he says he is. If he was who he says he is, I would be in heaven for a lifetime. He is caring, loving, mellow in personality, yet quite a strong man, from his writings. He is also humorous and a boy at heart. He is as his pictures show him to be. Unless two men can look the same and not be twins, it is an impossibility. Unfortunately, for me this is the case. If the real Uwe were single and had this caring, fun-loving nature and was mellow but strong—WOW! And if he spoke English (highly unlikely) because I don't know German—I would indeed be in heaven. Kinda forgot one important criterion: The real Uwe would have to fall in love with me as well (this is kinda a slim chance, especially since he doesn't know I even exist).

As for Lance? How many weeks can you reside in a hospital and not be sick? I understand about paying the bill before you are allowed to leave, BUT a month of being in a hospital? How do they expect to get paid if no one can leave? And being aware of the incident that caused them to go into the hospital doesn't really make sense.

I have asked Lance when we were discussing John, and I wonder what the answer would be. Is it true because someone states it is true (in regards to John's arrest)? How do you know when someone is telling you the truth if you have not seen them to look into their eyes to know? I asked him how he knew I was telling him the truth, and is it true just because it comes from my mouth or from my writings? His response in essence was: "Because I love you and believe you are telling me the truth." Why would I lie to him or he to me? Lance is a smooth talker, and it sounds like he means it. If there were such a man, I would be in heaven. I truly know I would be.

For a man to be so strong but so gentle, so strong but with so much feeling, so strong with no temper, so strong and so caring—

MMMMMMMMM—yup, I would be in heaven. Does such a man exist in reality for me with these qualities? Time will tell, but I no longer have that much time left.

Today Lance even tried to explain to me what went wrong in my current relationship and how we broke down in communication and how that was so sad to him. I will truly miss this man when I break ties with him—whoever he may be in reality. I still hope he is real but know from the internet and being told he isn't. You truly get caught up in a maze. For you it is reality, and for them? It is truly a fallacy. So sad but so true.

However, I did bring up to Lance that when I finally receive money, I will go to Nigeria to personally give him the money for the plane ticket. His reaction was precious. He was furious (especially for a man who claimed he never gets mad). He said I was treating him like child. Why do I need to go Nigeria? I should go to London and wait for him. He was upset that I did not have faith in his abilities to get out of Nigeria.

This was kinda what I was expecting but thought he would tell me not to go because I would be in jeopardy as he and his son were—BUT I did not expect the response that I was treating him like a child. I told him if he truly loved me, he wouldn't care how it happened. He should be caring about being out of the hospital and seeing me in person. I screamed at him for being childish about caring about some absurd reason and that wasn't what I thought he would say.

He didn't talk to me for two days.

It is kinda fun when you turn the tables on them because they don't want to see you. They have no intentions of seeing you. Because they aren't who you think they are.

Scamming the scammer worked for Lance because his reaction was not a reaction you would get under the normal circumstances if this was a real scenario.

As for John, scamming the scammer is not working. I can't get any of my money back this way.

CHAPTER 6

FEELING STUPID AFTER FINALLY REALIZING WHAT ACTUALLY OCCURRED AND HOW IT OCCURRED

WHEN I THINK BACK to John right now, I feel very stupid to have believed the lies and the doctoring of the pictures. However, back then I wasn't looking for deception such as that. I asked for pictures for proof, and I received pictures as proof. Never was I looking at them for deceit/deception. I looked at them for what I thought they were. Scammers are exceedingly clever, from my own experience, and then reading about them and what was done to Uwe Hubertus's pictures plus the overlays. What is still a puzzle is how they achieve to have conversations on web cameras of the person who is not the actual person. Truly masters of deception.

However, I did ask John's lawyer to write a contract that if anything happened to John in Germany, John's lawyer would pay me full restitution for the money I had given to John. I never just handed over the money. It was a loan. Just one problem with this: Ya gotta be real for the contract to be binding. DUH!

What I do know is if you don't break ties with the scammers, you will be driven mad with worry. There will always be a tragedy upon tragedy as there was for John. Look at the latest emails from John. We went from his son being sick to dying. Plus the tragedy that started happening to Lance. Who knows what the story for Lance would have been if I paid for the airline flight?

This is still very painful for me to write about because it is still going on, for one thing. For another, it is that I was deceived. Third, I questioned it, but there were always valid explanations that I believed. Lastly, I lost a ton of money and cannot explain how or why I gave it to John except that I did not want him injured or dead. I did not want to care more for money and the almighty dollar than I did a human life. In that moment of time, I truly believed his life and the life of his son were at stake.

I believe from my talks and readings AFTER the fact, the fear of losing the person they cared about or the person they care about is in some kind of danger/hardship is the reason that other victims have given money to their scammers as well. Others may have other reasoning for giving their money to the scammers. But whatever the reason for giving the money, it is because you fall prey to the scammer. The only way to stop the scammer from using you is to stop the contact even though you are drawn to them like bees to honey. To the victim, they are real people with real scenarios. Some scammers, from what I read on the web, will scare people into giving them the money with threats of harming the victims and the victims' loved ones. Luckily for me, that never happened, even though my reaction to threats is not the same.

The woman in the United States who sent the money, knowing full well what she was doing, fully believed that her scammer was truly in love with her and truly looked as he did on the internet. I asked her how she knew and how she was so positive that he was real, and she said she saw him through a web camera. I owe a lot to her because she really was the one who sent me on the quest and what caused me to write this book on scamming and my own personal experiences, even though this is truly embarrassing to do since in many aspects I feel like a gullible fool even though I don't consider myself such. But what I found out was the web camera pictures/videos are all faked to have you believe their incredible stories. I actually talked to a young boy. I heard this young boy's voice plead with me to help his father, who had fallen sick, and he did not know what to do for his father since he was by himself when his father suddenly collapsed. I heard the young boy tell me his father (John) was not moving. This, too, was faked. Are they truly teaching their young to do this same thing at an early age? I learned a lot.

Just wish I knew the woman who sent Lance money on my first go around with scammers and not my second go-around. I would have saved a lot of money. But hopefully, I am saving your money for those of you who are reading this book and have not been scammed to date or for those who are being scammed. As you read this book, wake up and stop what you are doing. As I stated earlier, I feel very gullible at believing everything that was told to me even though I wasn't 100 percent sure when I sent the money because at the time it sounded as though there was a real need, and I feared their lives were in danger. However, I am not the only gullible person. There have been websites set up like the one for Uwe Hubertus to protect his name because a lot of women fell deeply in love with him and they, too, wanted to help him any way they could. Same with John's face. Whomever the real face belongs to is yet to be determined by me. Plus we have the face of the man the woman sent the money to in Nigeria. She fell in love with that man and truly believes he is real and has for years. She gives him more than nine hundred dollars per month since she has known him. She lives in a house with no light or gas in order to give him this amount. How many others are there?

However, for the woman who sent the money to Lance— who truly is worse—is it the scammer or the woman who is full aware of the scam and sends the money to the scammer with full knowledge of her wrongful acts, then decides if there is a second request for money to inform the people who are being scammed that they were scammed because she fears her scammer may love someone else? This to me is worse BECAUSE she could have informed the people being scammed prior to the first send, OR if she couldn't find them on the web to never pick up the money from the MoneyGram places. Why send the initial funds? This is for you to answer. I have my own assumptions on this topic.

Today I had a young woman say 'HI' to me on the internet. I am sure she is a scammer as well, but I am ignoring it. I do admit I have a soft heart and really care about people and will cry in a heartbeat at anyone's sad story—real or fake. BUT first do the investigation before you send any money to anyone (male, female, old or young) and ensure they are real. Spend the money and go and see them before you send any money. If they say you can't do it because they are at some remote sites, then don't do it—just DON'T. I just wish I did the legwork on my first scammer. I did but apparently not well enough. I skimmed but did not research. RESEARCH if you must, but better yet, DON'T—JUST DON'T. Listen to this old fool and learn from my mistakes.

So, I guess I lost about one hundred fifty thousand dollars this year that I have to explain to the IRS and pay taxes for money I never personally used. This is coupled with all of the penalties of withdrawing from my IRA account early. FUN, FUN, FUN..

I have lost weight, but the good part to this is I have been given compliments out the wazoo because of the weight loss. I have had people just out of the blue hug me and kiss me (haven't quite figured that out. The only explanation I can give to that is when you are in love, I think you have a special aura about you that others are attracted to—OR I am exuding a pheromone). This happened to me in my thirties and forties. Somehow I missed it through my fifties, and now, when I am in my sixties, this is happening again? Kinda old for this. BUT I will be going with the flow, hopefully a little wiser. I won't stop worrying about people, but don't take me as a target, either—I learned a lot.

If this book only gets read by a few people, I hope you learned a little from my mistakes. Please, I know our hearts go out to people who are suffering and have injustices done, but for your own sanity and if someone says HELLO on Facebook and you don't know them—DON'T RESPOND. IF you do, hone up to it because you may be going on a very dangerous ride. If your health is impaired, it could end, and I am serious because I have worried and spent many a sleepless night and didn't eat because of worry. If I had a bad heart, I think it would have been the end of me.

If you really think about it, you fell in love—you really did (you did; the scammer did not). This really isn't much different than giving your spouse money to go through college, then he/she dumps you after you pay for their college tuition/books/etc. You slave working several jobs while they (he/she) just go to school, and when they are finally completed with their coursework and eventually graduate, they soon after apply for a divorce. The only difference is you went through your bankroll a lot quicker, got no perks, and got screwed quicker than a person taking college courses to earn their degree.

Places that I thought should be better at resolving these issues should do it better than they have been doing and be a little proactive. If they are short staffed, we should place/give more resources to them because this is a growing crime. The Facebook site that the constituents set up for Uwe Hubertus has one hundred thirty-eight members, and they have closed the group.

Plus, the banks scammers are using for their scams should be more aware of this, and their fraud department should answer emails sent to them. Plus, I called them on several occasions to verbally ask them about the screens and inform them of what was going on, and the responses I received were not the responses I was expecting. It seemed as though they didn't care. I sent the link to them that was sent to me for the account information. Their name and reputation are also at stake because by not paying attention to it, it gives the crime and fraudulent acts credibility. This should be addressed.

Banks especially should ensure that the screens with their names are legitimate when their reputation is involved. Another interesting thing I found out about telephone numbers throughout this entire scenario is that the telephone companies can't tell you if a phone number that is out of country phone number was used in this country or another country. The U. S. code is 011. So, if a call was prefaced by 011, was it used in this country or dialed in another country? The reason, you ask? Well, sometimes I received a call from 234, which is a Nigeria number, and other times it was prefaced by 011234. The question was: Is it being used in the United States if no code of 011 was used and out of the country if 011 was used as a preface to the 234? No one was able to answer this question, which didn't seem that difficult to me. They went on the internet to find the answer. This baffled me as well. I can honestly say as of this I still don't know, but I am assuming that the 011 is when they are truly out of the U.S. dialing into the U.S. However, the calls I received from London did not have a preface of 011.

CHAPTER 7

FINALLY MEETING OTHERS WHO WERE ALSO SCAMMED

I FINALLY CONNECTED TO the group that was formed for eliminating scammers from Facebook and met some incredible women and a man who welcomed me to the group. He welcomed me by saying:

"Welcome to the group, and please contribute as you can. You will find articles about romance scamming and the emotional effect of being scammed in the 'file section,' and lots of very good educational videos about scammers is found on YouTube (just type in romance scammers, and you'll get a very quick education). Here you will find help in the group with your education on the traps and schemes of the internet predators, mentoring, and guidance in your recovery, and a place where you can post and expose internet scammers as you find and identify them."

"Here we accept you without judgment or recriminations, and we ask you do the same with each new member who comes after you but remember that this is an anti-scam site and that is its mission; it is not a social site. Infighting with other members is not allowed, and you must understand that our members have been victims of these internet predators (scammers), are at different stages in their recovery, and may need different help or guidance from each of us."

"If you have a question, just ask it in the group, and we will respond with an answer and help you. Or feel free to PM one of the administrators for help."

This was indeed very sweet of them to care, and they care because they, too, experienced it. It is nice to know you are not alone, but it is also scary that there are many groups on Facebook that are anti-scammers. WHY IS IT SCARY? Because that means the problem is larger than I thought. Where is the money going that we give to the scammers? Is it funding their clothes, food, children, expensive cars? OR is it funding something else, such as guns and weapons against us? Does anyone really know? Should we be finding out? Another scammer wrote the following:

If the essence of my being has caused a smile to have appeared upon your face or a touch of joy within your heart, then in living I have made my mark.

I stole it and placed it on my website to see how many responses I would get, and was I surprised. I received more responses and likes than I ever received before on anything. They know how to attract and what to take and copy—they just do.

One of the anti-scammers found yet another Uwe Hubertus scammer named Mark, who wrote:

Mark Member M556618 55, Leyton, London

I am a fun, loving, independent and honest man who is looking for the same thing in a woman. I like every simple things in life such as; travelling, swimming, fishing, camping,, sports and walking along the beach front. I have been single for 5 years without any serious relationship; I will like to meet a woman who dreams of bringing two hearts together as one.

I believe this was from a dating site. I personally believe dating sites are dangerous chances for love. It can work, but your chances are slim. Best to go out and live life and not be someone who hopes that some miracle will happen, and the love of your life will just appear. They are great for a friendship, but I have learned not to give anything to them, **especially your heart,** if you have not met them. Besides the money or items you gave away—or rather I gave away—I also gave my heart (the most precious gift you can give anyone) to two men and got emotionally involved in their lives. The heart—oh, the heart. Nothing is more devastating than giving your heart away, thinking it would be protected and cared for by that person, and then to have it suddenly smashed into wee tiny pieces.

From another member of the Facebook group, I learned of the term "AVATAR," which is a virtual world from the site http:// en.wikipedia. org/wiki/Second_Life.

The definition of it is the following:

Second Life is an online virtual world, developed by Linden Lab (a company based in San Francisco) and launched on June 23, 2003; and which in 2014 has about 1 million regular users, according to Linden Lab, who owns Second Life. In many ways, Second Life is similar to MMORPGs (Massively Multiplayer Online Role-Playing Games), Linden Lab is emphatic that their creation is not a game: "There is no manufactured conflict, no set objective. "

The virtual world can be accessed freely via Linden Labs' own client Programs, or via alternative third-party viewers. Second Life users create virtual representations of themselves, called avatars (also called residents), and they are able to interact with other avatars, places, or objects. They can explore the world (known as the grid), meet other residents, socialize, participate in individual and group activities, and build, create, shop, and trade virtual Property and services with one another. It is a Platform that Principally features 3D-based user-generated content. SL also had its own virtual currency—the Linden Dollar—which was exchangeable with real-world currency. Second Life is intended for people aged sixteen and over, with the exception of thirteen- to fifteen-year-old users restricted to the Second Life region of a sponsoring institution (e.g., school). Built into the software is a three-dimensional modeling tool based on simple geometric shapes that allows residents to build virtual objects. There is also a procedural scripting language—Linden Scripting Language— which can be used to add interactivity to objects. Sculpted prims (sculpties), mesh, textures for clothing or other objects, animations, and gestures can be created using external software and then imported The Second Life terms of service Provide that users retain copyright for any content they create, and the server and client Provide simple digital rights management (DRM) functions. However, Linden Lab changed their terms of service in August 2013 to be able to use user-generated content for any Purpose. The new terms of service Prevent users from using textures from third-party texture services, as some of them Pointed out explicitly. Users can also Photograph in Second Life with the camera technology the client programs have.

http://en.wikipedia.org/wiki/Second_Life

However, the person who belongs to the anti-scammers group described Soldier Avatar as:

An AVATAR is using a PICTURE belonging to SOMEONE ELSE OTHER THAN THE SENDER.

I have found that people who assist the scammers in their scams, such as the women who send money to the scammers from other women and get some restitution for doing so, are called mules. Why MULES? 1 have no idea.

Here is something I grabbed from one of the victim's scammers of Uwe:

WARNING: SCAMMERS HAVE IN THEIR POSSESSION A RECORD WEBCAM OF UWE!! IF YOU "SEE HIM ON CAM", IT IS NOT UWE "LIVE" YOU ARE SEEING, BUT A RECORDING. IF YOU ASK A SCAMMER TO WRITE YOUR NAME ON A PAPER AND SHOW IT IN CAMERA, HE WILL REFUSE, OR HIS CAM WILL "BREAK" RIGHTAT THIS MOMENT.

ALSO, UWE IS NOT A MILITARY MAN, HE IS A CIVILIAN. ALL PICTURES OF HIM IN THE UNFORM IS A PHOTOSHOP

One woman, for whatever reason, is really worried about me psychologically and wrote this to me:

Beverly, I am CONCERNED over BOTH your PHYSICAL, as well as your EMOTIONAVSPIRITUAL, well-being; & ALTHOUGH, you are a RESILIENT & highly CAPABLE Woman, the PSYCHOPATHY

that EXISTS among these CRIMINALS can be FORMIDABLE!! THEREFORE, as long as CONTACT with these MISCREANTS is maintained by you—you REMAIN VERY VULNERABLE!! AND, THE FBI CYBER CRIME DIVISIONIS OVERLOADED, & who KNOWS WHEN they would contact you!! THEREFORE, you are remaining IMPRISONED via FORCING yourself to CONTINUE this FALSE relationship with this CRIMINAL!!

Additionally, since he is NOT in this country, how could he be APPREHENDED, ESPECIALLY with his COUNTRY'S CORRUPT reigning government, right?

Sweetie., a VITAL aspect of BEING EMOTIONALLY HEALED, following a LOSS, or TRAUMA, is ACCEPTANCE... acceptance of WHAT one can, or cannot CONTROL. Multiple THOUSANDS of SCAMMING VICTIMS. ATTEMPTING to do exactly what you are doing, have thus far, come up against a GLASS WALL... therefore, BEV please attempt to look at this DIFFICULT situation in terms of your CONTINUED HEALING... & keep your FOCUS UPON YOU, & UNDERSTANDING THE inner forces & life experiences, which might have predisposed you, into entering into this DEVALUING Scenario.

Although I know she is trying to help me, she has sent me many, many messages informing me over and over again, which makes me feel that she is still under the psychological control of her scammer in many ways. Psychologically, I have released these men. Once you know you are being scammed, it is easy to release the psychological hold they have on you—at least it was for me. Everyone is different. Some will never release the hold the scammer has on them. However, I now understand the trauma and effect it has on one's psyche, and it is indeed formidable. It is not to be taken lightly or dismissed. It is easy to dismiss from the outside looking in. It has a cult-like effect on you. This cannot be denied.

The same person who was concerned for me also wrote this later in the same day:

I STRONGLY SUSPECT THAT PROFILE PHONEY... CALLS HIMSELF; PETER NAHAR NAHAR. CONTACTED ME ON FACEBOOK MESSENGER, CALLING ME DEAR, ASKING ME TO FRIEND ME, SINCE AYAGE REMINDS HIM OF HIS MOTHER, & WANTING TO FIND FRIENDS OF JESUS CLAIMS TO WORK AS LAB TECHNICIAN IN SAUDI ARABIA, ONE DAUGHTER. HATES BEING THERE. WANTS TO LEAVE THERE. WARNING SIGNS for me:

(1) WHEN ASKED, HE repeatedly IGNORES answering QUESTIONS of WHAT CITY HE LIVES IN, THE CURRENT TIME THERE, what COMPANY HE WORKS FOR... HE IGNORES answering these QUESTIONS.

(2) I ASKED HIM HIS DAILY DUTIES AS LAB TECH... IGNORED ANSWERING this question, also. I even asked a specialty-related question that a LAB TECH SHOULD KNOW, & ignores answering this, also.

(3) SUSPECT SCAMMER ATTEMPTS to SWAY ME using 'GUILT', stating that I RUINED HIS EVENING' by DOUBTING HIM, & by acting like 'POLICE'. AGAIN, when I politely again explain that I needed REASSURANCE of his probable identity via his ANSWERING my SIMPLE QUESTIONS, he CONTINUED AVOIDING ANSWERING my simple questions. DOES ANYONE KNOW PIC... NAME? 1 WILL PUT THROUGH 'PIGBUSTERS'_ HOWEVER, for ME, WITH the WARNING SIGNS, I AM COMFORTABLE BLOCKING HIM.

This in essence tells me she is still out there being contacted and not following the advice she gave to me earlier in the day. IF someone says HI and you don't know them, ignore them. By you responding back with a HI, you are supporting them in their endeavors. Just move on with your life. IF you befriended them, then block them upon the word HI—TRUST ME! IF contacted by someone you don't know, normally they don't send you personal messages right away—they send public messages. What she wrote above is WHAT NOT TO DO! Block and do something else to get them out of your mind, no matter what they look like or how cute the message was initially. Take a walk, go out with friends, sit in a park, go shopping—anything to not focus on that person. The above person is playing with fire.

Recently, I found that her boyfriend passed five months ago and most of her family has died. This must have been such a trauma for her to go through, and then to be victimized by a scammer. This is a crime for anyone to do such a thing to an already emotionally distraught human. Scammers have no feelings for you or what they do to you financially. It is all about their survival and their needs. Understand that. People who have been victimized try to make some sense of the situation. To be honest, there isn't any sense to it—plain and simple. It is just about the scammer's needs and wants. You are a means to an end. I have since found out she has a medical degree and worries about the psychological wellbeing of all who were scammed. Her heart is very kind. However, having a kind heart makes you an easy target for scammers.

Yet another woman who got scammed by a Uwe Hubertus imposter wrote this:

Yes this Uwe Scammers are very dynamic I know have meet one ... this Uwe are living in Germany and it's a woman from Denmark have create this site for support to the real Uwe she have meet him to for real... what is so scary in this that are the scamming growing more and more... every dating site have scammers on their members and all scammers going around all over... if they get deleted and blocked the go to next site... here they only change names and place of living but same faces everywhere they are.

I wrote a complaint to the FBI a year ago, but they have not responded. I heard that the FBI does not bother to respond if the amount that you lost is under one hundred thousand dollars.

This last statement is just sad if it is true. For the FBI not to care if anyone has a loss under one hundred thousand dollars is despicable. However, I lost over one hundred thousand, and I have never been contacted to date.

Someone was impersonating a general, and people were scammed by him. The following comment is from one of the ones who was scammed:

Last year I was "scammed" by the false james terry. I tried to keep in touche •with the real general and I informed him that his pic was stolen, he never answered back, never...

You'd think a general would care that his face is being used to scam people out of their money, but apparently it is not enough. However, he may not have taken her seriously and dismissed it. People will continue to scam until they are stopped. The scammers know that by the time law enforcement acts on it, they (the scammers) will be long gone and onto another victim. If the law enforcement bodies acted quickly, then most would be caught. People think they would never be stupid to fall for this, but it isn't stupidity that gets you into the web of a scammer. It is a casual conversation for starters. Then you start to talk as you would to a friend. They find out what you are about and what you care about, and then it starts, and you don't even realize it until you are into it.

Thus, the web has begun. They are smooth.

I received a number for the FBI in Washington, D.C., and I called it on August 11, 2014. For online crime, they inform you to go online to IC3.gov and follow directions. The phone number then automatically hung up after making this declaration. This was not what I wanted to hear. So being a stubborn cuss that I am, I then redialed and got a person, who informed me that I needed to call a local number. I took down the number and I called it. Surprise! It didn't work. They said it was out of service. SSSSOOOO I called for a third time (some say the third time is a charm, and apparently it is) and got an agent, who informed me that I needed to enter the information on IC3.gov, and I told her I did that several months ago. She asked if I received a confirmation number, and I stated I did. She told me to quit contacting because they would get quite intimidating, and I told her I understood but I wanted the damn son-of-a-bitch caught. She said I could be placing myself in jeopardy, and I told her I understood that as well. I told her they were doing it in the United States using major banks as their vehicle and there were so many men and women being taken. I also told her I understood that my money might never be recuperated, but if I were to catch them, it would be worth the loss to me—and to be honest, IF this were my last act on this earth, that would be okay with me.

The email IC3 sent me when I made the original complaint was the following:

Thank you for filing a complaint with the Internet Crime Complaint Center (IC3).

This is the only reply you will receive from the IC3. Because we receive thousands of complaints per week, •we cannot reply to every complaint received or to every request for updates.

However, once we forward your complaint to investigators in the field, they may contact you for further information. Consequently, it is important that you maintain any evidence you have relating to your complaint. Evidence can include canceled checks, credit card receipts, Phone bills, mailing envelopes, mail receipts, Printed copies of websites, copies of emails, or similar items.

If you wish to view, download, or add information to your complaint, go to http://complaint.ic3.gov/update and log in with the following: Complaint Id: 11405011726492112

Well, I received the above email with a complaint ID on May 1, 2014, and it is now August. So, all of May, all of June, all of July, and halfway through August, and nothing. It was not what I was expecting when I originally filed the complaint. I was kinda hoping for a quicker response.

Then to add insult to injury, we have sites being advertised all over the internet for online dating. Talk about asking for trouble. See below:

Have You Tried Online Dating Yet?

It's never been easier to meet smart, attractive singles online. Could you meet your soul mate today? Find Your Perfect Match Now »

Still advice from another anti-scamming site:

If you see these texts, or parts of them in messages, then you are dealing with a scammer, probably from West Africa or Malaysia, but may be from other countries as well. Scammers use cut and pasted text because they are usually almost illiterate, uneducated, and have little English, or because it is easier to do it when dealing with hundreds of potential victims a day. Note: scammers hardly ever address you by name and this is because it makes it unnecessary to edit messages with names in them. They will call you "Honey", "Baby", "my Queen", "Angel", etc.

***Never** tell a scammer how you caught him*. Never tell him about his message text and never correct his mistakes. We like our scammers to continue to be uneducated and stupid. Remember when a message suggests you send money, you are talking to a scammer and whatever the excuse he gives you, send nothing and leave without a word.*

*Even if you think you are dealing with a woman be assured it is a boy in an internet café.

Be careful with the people, 'Who suddenly contact you on SKYPE/MSN/Yahoo messenger. There are NO SOLDIERS, GENERALS, SERGEANTS or OFFICERS, using messengers who will offer you romance, especially if they claim to be in Afghanistan, Libya, Syria etc.

Offshore:

***ENGINEERS, GOLD AND GEMSTONE DEALERS**, and similar persons are also **FAKE**.*

<u>*Take notice:*</u>

SOLDIERS NEVER PAY FOR LEAVE *Government Departments DO NOT USE WESTERN UNION/ MoneyGram, or similar transfers.*

@@@@@@@@@@@@@@@@@@@@@@@@@@@@@

This is a SCAM! DO NOT RESPOND!

@@@@@@@@@@@@@@@@@@@@@@@@@@@@@

The anti-scamming sites eliminated my scammer site on Facebook. Lance did not seem like a happy camper. He has called me four times today, and I accidentally answered before I looked at the number. The number is a Nigerian number. For anyone who does not know, Nigerian numbers start with a 234 prefix. I believe I previously mentioned the prefix, but in case I did not, please take note of it. Lance stated he wrote to me on Facebook. I told him it appeared that his Facebook name is no longer there because I tried to send him a message and it was no longer active. The interesting thing he told me is he sent me an email. I asked him where he sent it to, and he said Gmail. Why is this so interesting, you ask? WELL, I never sent him an email from my GMAIL account. I sent it to John but NEVER LANCE... Hmm... My GMAIL name is completely different than any other email I have. SOO the question that goes unanswered is: How did he get my GMAIL name? and for a man who tells me he never gets mad, he was quite upset when he called me. He said he loved me but could not get to me when he called or emailed. I asked him why he sent it to my GMAIL. Lance then told me he replied to an email I sent him. REALLY? Something wasn't right, but my question was HOW?

Lance once again contacted me on GMAIL, informing me that he was unable to contact me through Facebook and he created a new account. I did try to see if I could find it, and I could not. I'm not sure how Facebook blocks the user who is reported as scamming. Here is the email Lance sent to me on GMAIL:

I can't get into mg Facebook still don't know what happened so I opened a new one and have sent you series of messages I don't know why you are not getting my them still trying to figure out why you aren't getting my messages... just look for La Mu... that's what I used in setting up the new Facebook... love and missing you terrible...

But you have to remember that this person is not who they are. Never think they are, or you will still be in their web.

I'm still not sure how the anti-scamming websites think reporting the users as scammers on Facebook will work on a permanent basis. This seems like the never-ending story and a circle to me. But again, I do not know how the inner workings of the anti-scammer sites really work. I see the group reporting the scammers, but that is all I see. But if Lance is indeed able to open another Facebook account, then what purpose does it serve? It delays the scammer for a short period of time, but the scammer still will contact the mark (so to speak) as Lance did with me.

In addition, the anti-scammers got a virus from one of the members because they stated she was a mule. She loved her scammer more than the group and stated to the scammers what the group was doing. The scammers then started to send out viruses to the members, and they were bombarded with friendship requests.

This should tell you this is a serious crime, and the effects can be devastating.

Again, to me, this is a crime. Affecting the computers by viruses is malicious. It is the scammers feeling the need to retaliate and to do harm to those who are trying to stop them. However, how far are the scammers willing to go to protect their business of scamming?

SSSSOOOOOO...

BASELINE: Be careful. Scammers are experts in their field, and as long as we support them, they will exist. They are great actors as well. They really make you feel they are who they say they are. However, PLEASE know they aren't real. The situations that are tearing you apart emotionally aren't real. NOTHING IS REAL—EXCEPT YOUR EMOTIONS.

Scammers learn how to create illusions to make you believe they are telling you the truth. This affects BOTH men and women. BOTH are vulnerable—BOTH. It isn't a sexist thing. It is an emotional thing. The emotional hold is strong. The scammers have it down to a fine art. Be careful of viruses that may be sent to you as well if you let them know your email address. Just BE CAREFUL! Did 1 say "be careful" a lot? SSSOOO BE CAREFUL!

CHAPTER 8

MOVING ON

I HAVE REALIZED THROUGH this entire writing that I was missing something in my life, and for this reason I thank my scammers. Not for making me broke. I will never than them for that, but I will thank them for making me realize I was in a rut. I needed something I was missing, apparently something I needed and wanted desperately, and one of the reasons I, initially, gave them the money.

I wanted romance—well, maybe a little more than romance. I want the entire love package. I want the courtship, the love, the tenderness, the romance, and finally to be married. I never have been; I've been scared shitless of making the fatal error that would last a lifetime. For me it would be a lifetime because I am only doing the wedding thing once. Plain and simple. I reached a point in my life that I thought I was just waiting for the end to come. My mom passed away at sixty-four and my dad at sixty-nine. Both were still young. I am sixty-two now and since longevity doesn't seem to be in my genes, I have decided to live life to the fullest. I have decided to leave my significant other of twenty-six years. I don't feel he is happy in life any more than I am. It will free him as well.

When we first met, we had a blast. I was more fun to be with back then. I want that me back. SO I decided to move out of the house I shared with my significant other and once again live on my own. I need to find me before sharing my life with someone else. If my significant other and I were meant to be together, we would have gotten married by now. We talked about it in the years but always dismissed it. WHY? My guess is it wasn't meant to be.

I have bought a vacation package to Hawaii (one destination) Mexico (another destination), Vegas (still another destination), and lastly ending in Florida. HEY, I'm not quite over yet. I have the option of a cruise—yes, a weight-gaining cruise.

Will I be happy? Time will tell. But one thing is for DAMN sure: I will LIVE the rest of my remaining days.

For the reason of the scammers giving me a wakeup call, I am thankful to them. I have a life to live and I have a love for life, so look out, world, 'cause I feel totally liberated. It doesn't matter if I find MR. RIGHT. What matters is that I find the old me. The me I loved.

I also realized by talking to friends, I am not the only one living a life of complacency. Why do we live a life that we aren't happy with? I am not saying to leave your spouse. But if you love your spouse—truly love them—then stir it up with romance. Wear that sexy see-through nightgown and talk dirty/sexy to your mate. Grab them, pull them toward you, kiss them passionately, and see what happens. It may be just the thing you needed to do in order to stir it up again and revive feelings that were asleep. If nothing happens— well, you may want to really think about your life and make some changes to it. We worry about finances and how we will make it on our own, but we are willing to give money to the scammer? Doesn't make sense.

If I didn't make myself clear—do I want tons of men? HELL NO. I want just one. A very special one to pop into my life. However, if I never meet him, will I be happy? Yes, I think so, because I found me. Knowing who you are and not getting lost in other people's lives is the key.

For other people, it may not be romance—just don't get snookered into a scamming situation no matter how heart-wrenching it is. NO SEE IN PERSON, NO GIVE. THE FIRST AND ONLY RULE. GOT IT?

SO to all of the scammers who may be reading my book, thank you for waking me up. For all of the women you hurt financially and mentally? I wish you burn in hell—LITERALLY!

CHAPTER 9

HARD LESSON LEARNED

THIS HAS BEEN A learning experience for me that I paid dearly for in order to acquire the knowledge. Please learn from me and not from the actual scammer. Please learn from my mistakes, and please don't make your own mistakes. Hopefully, I gave you enough insight and websites to do further investigation on your own. Plus, IF you get caught in a web or you are unsure you are in a web, call the FBI or contact IC3—or join an anti-scammer site and ask your questions of them. For the people who love to be scammed in **hopes** that one day you will meet this person who loves you so much, there is nothing anyone will be able to tell you to break you free. If you feel like living in poverty and never having a sexual encounter with the love of your life, that this is the way you want to live, and/ or never kissing his/her lips isn't enough of a wakeup call, then sorry—I'm not sure you can be helped. It is those people I really feel sorry for because they are truly lost.

I prefaced the book on a few items, and I will end it the same way.

1. If you think you are being scammed, then take it you ARE being scammed and terminate all modes of communication with that person. If the thought even remotely crosses your mind, then trust that feeling. Just terminate the relationship no matter how painful it is to do because in the end the pain will be magnified to very gut wrenching and you will also be BROKE. DON'T ASK the scammer if he is a scammer. He will deny it vehemently and not in a negative way but a "soft-spoken I am telling the truth" way. Break ties early in the game (and a game it is

to them and you are the pawn). The longer you stay with it, the deeper you will get and the harder it is to break free. NO SEE IN PERSON, THEN NO GIVE.

2. Intrigue: IF you don't listen to item number one, then you will be taken on an incredible emotional ride. There will be a lot of passion that you feel for the person. There will be mounds and mounds of tears shed for them because you actually believe the tales being told, and trust me, the stories are tales and NOT reality. Your heart will be torn to pieces, and in the end you will be BROKE. Did 1 say "BROKE" in item one and item two? YES! BROKE! HMMMMM... That alone should stop you dead from communicating.

3. ROMANCE. YES! YES! And **YES!** They will romance you. Write very romantic poetry that will take your breath away and make you say, "OH, WOW." You will engage the romantic side of you and bring back feelings that you thought you lost or were hidden. They will be able to read you from what you tell them and play it to the fullest they can. They will send you pictures of themselves (not actually them, but you will receive pictures of the person you believe to be them). They will show pictures of their children, of themselves at theatres, at plays, on camera, and even on video cams. But you must remember, it isn't real. Until you actually meet someone, it isn't real. You really don't know that person on the other side of the PC. YOU REALLY DON'T. This is the hard part because you have become very close friends with someone with whom you shared your life. You have truly fallen in love and will do just about anything within your power for them because you love them that much. BUT (always a but) ask yourself somewhere along the line: What have they done for me? NOTHING besides romance you. They haven't given you anything but a romantic ride that will lead to tragedy. They will come up with so many lines and comebacks that will truly make your head spin. But have they made passionate love to you? NO! You have nothing but a mind game. Realize early on that you will never meet them.

IF you truly want romance—and we really, secretly or not so secretly, all do—why do I say that? We write the romantic poetry, we read the romantic poetry, we write romantic books, we read romantic books, seductive books like *Fifty Shades of Grey* (by the way, *Fifty*

Shades of Grey doesn't hold a candle to what a scammer can and will say to make you want to crawl out of your skin), we write romantic songs, we sing romantic songs, we love receiving flowers at the office or at home—we search for it all the time. We sometimes find the perfect mate who does the same, but unless you do it over and over again and never lose the feeling you felt when you first met the perfect mate, it dies. YOU BOTH HAVE TO ROMANCE EACH OTHER UNTIL YOU DIE. Once you lose the romantic feeling, it is hard for it to come back for that same person. LANCE was so right when he said to be each other's best friend and NEVER go to bed angry at the one you love. Plus, he said to always make it fresh and new by trying things you never did before.

Anger festers and destroys love. When one does romantic gestures and the other doesn't do the romancing anymore, then the one who is doing the romancing will eventually give it up as well.

IF you are currently by yourself and have no one, please go out and enjoy a dinner by yourself at a fancy or maybe not-so-fancy restaurant. Order something you would never order and maybe have a glass of wine or two even if you can't afford it. You were giving your money to a scammer when you couldn't afford it, and the cost was greater. Aren't you worth the special treatment every once in a while? Plus, you never know who you may meet. Maybe it isn't at a restaurant—maybe a walk on the beach or just walking the street or even in a grocery store (I remember a few times when someone came running to me in a parking lot after I bought groceries and asking me out on a date since he saw me shopping there other times. I had someone I loved very much at the time and never took him up on it). It is not the place you meet—it is if you are open to the experience. Plus, it is easier opening up to someone you haven't seen or met because you are shy or whatever your reasons are and being able to keep the scammer as just a friend isn't going to work—trust me, it isn't. BECAUSE no matter what, somewhere along the lines of communication your emotions will get the best of you.

Maybe romance isn't your thing. Maybe it is religion, or travels, or a combo of things, or whatever. The scammer will find your weakness and play you like you have never been played before.

4. This is the last thing and the thing we like to do the most. WE BLAME OTHERS. we blame the scammers for what they did to us. UH, they didn't do it; we did it to ourselves. No one held a gun to our heads, no one forced us to do anything we at the time didn't want to do. We did it with full conviction that we were helping someone who needed the help at the time. We loved that person so much—that was what we cared about at the time, to help them in their time of need. We feel outrage when it dawns on us finally that we were taken to the cleaners, so to speak. We now realize it was all under false pretenses that we did what we did. But is it the scammer's fault or ours for being so gullible?

NOW I am not saying we should not go after them and prosecute them for what they did because what they did and are doing is very wrong—so very wrong. The pain and agony you feel is beyond belief. They should be prosecuted to the fullest extent of the law because they prey on people and sometimes for victims like Uwe Hubertus. They did not ask him for money. What they did to him was to use him in order for their scam to work. This man is exceedingly handsome, but his face is all over the internet with so many names attached to it—it is unbelievable. Uwe Hubertus had women actually travel to him to meet him face to face. He had to explain to the women that he wasn't who they thought he was. This is the biggest crime because this poor, sweet man has done nothing wrong.

I am not condoning the scammer at all—I think and wish the ones who scammed me are caught—but I also know I did what I did because I wanted no harm to come to a very sweet man and his son (not real, but I didn't know that at the time). I can't blame someone else for my actions. I wish I could, but I can't. I should have researched better. I had some doubts and should have listened to my doubts. This is very hard to explain to someone who has not been scammed. It is easy to say what to do and not do if outside of the scamming realm. If I was not caught up in it myself, my reactions and advice would have been different from what I actually did. I am going to add item number five to my list.

5. Don't try to scam a scammer. I am trying to do this, but there is always an out for them. I would feel great if I could because even

though it will never equal what I gave, it would give me a little piece of satisfaction. However, scamming a scammer keeps you in the web. It is better to have the people who are supposed to handle this handle this. This book is also being written to hopefully attract attention to this growing problem and maybe give more resources to the agencies that are supposed to help/assist people with this issue. I think I will accept my losses, take it that the law enforcement groups are not going to help me in time for them to catch my scammers, and actually take my own advice and sever ties with my scammers. This, too, is a hard lesson to learn.

I hope this gave you some insight and hopefully understanding of what goes on when being scammed. AND I will pray that you don't fall prey to them EVER in your lifetime. Remember, the scams can be elaborate or small, one scammer or a group of them to back the other. A scam is scam is a scam. IF you haven't met them, be thankful. IF you have, please ignore them—or better yet block them. They are persistent and great actors—actually fantastic actors. PLUS, the face you see is not their face. PLEASE understand that part. And above all, remember the internet sites and support groups, and IF you find a scammer, please REPORT, REPORT, REPORT! Did I say "REPORT"? **REPORT'. Still not sure if you were scammed after all of this? Join an anti-scamming group and ask them. They have it down pat. They will look the person up and inform you if he/she is a scammer, and the group will shut the scammer down very quickly. It is not hard to find an anti-scamming group.**

CHAPTER 10

GOVERNMENT AGENCIES FOR FILING COMPLAINTS

AN INTERNET SITE FOR filing a complaint for online crimes is: http://www.ic3. gov/default.aspx

The IC3 accepts online internet crime complaints from either the actual victim or from a third party to the complainant. They can best process your complaint if they receive accurate and complete information from you. Therefore, they request that you provide the following information when filing a complaint:

- Your name

- Your mailing address

- Your telephone number

- The name, address, telephone number, and web address, if available, of the individual or organization you believe defrauded you

- Specific details on how, why, and when you believe you were defrauded

- Any other relevant information you believe is necessary to support your complaint

Other websites for filing complaints are:

http://www.interpol.int/

http://www.ic3. gov/crimeschemes.aspx

http://atg.wa.gov/wirescams.aspx

http://www.secretservice.gov/faq.html

Or call:

(202) 324-3000 (MAIN FBI HEADQUARTERS IN WASHINGTON, D.C.)

Another helpful site:

http://www.datingnm ore.com/fraud/scam_blacklist.htm

Nigerian scams come in many forms, including the 419 scam, when they offer to transfer millions of dollars into your bank account, or the lottery scam, when they tell you that you've won something in some bogus lottery.

However, the **Nigerian dating scam (or romance scam),** besides just asking for money for their studies, sick relatives, etc., usually involves this scheme: The scammers upload fake attractive photos—in most cases, of white people. They pretend to be the foreign specialists working in Nigeria or Ghana (usually originally from the U.S. and UK, but it may also be Canada, Australia, or any other European country.)

After they establish some lovely correspondence with you, fall in love and maybe even send a couple of cheap presents, they will either:

a) be almost on their way to meet you, but something will happen to them: They will get robbed, beaten, get into the hospital, or some other misfortune will happen, and of course, you will be their only contact to ask for financial help, or:

b) tell you their employer pays them with money orders and they can't cash them in Nigeria. They will send you the money orders and ask you to deposit them into your bank account and then wire the money to them via Western Union. Usually, they say to keep some money for your trouble. Needless to say, those money orders are no good and not even worth the paper they're printed on. If you cash them or deposit them into your account, money orders will come back after a few weeks as fraudulent, and you will be responsible for paying back the money to the bank and sometimes even charged for passing a counterfeit instrument. There is also a reshipping scam, when they will ask you to reship goods for them. These goods are purchased with stolen credit cards. Never reship anything for strangers, especially to Africa. There is a reason why online merchants usually don't ship there.

There are also military scams (for God's sake, there are NO American generals browsing dating sites, and NO military man will EVER ask you for money. Then there is a recovery scam: a scammer re-contacting you pretending to be FBI, EFCC, or any other authority, telling he can help you recover your money—but for a fee, of course.

And finally, there is a "stuck parcel" scam, when they supposedly sent you goods/gifts, but they got stuck somewhere on the way (for example, at customs), and you have to pay to "customs"/bogus shipping company to get them. All types of scams are described in details on Romance scam.

Please remember: white people in Nigeria or Ghana contacting you on the dating sites or so call networks are always 100% scam. No exceptions. There are no white engineers or female models stranded there. It is always scam. Once you stop giving it a benefit of doubt like newbies sometimes do, you will be safe.

When we say "Nigerian scam", it doesn't mean it originates from Nigeria only. It may also originate from any other West African country, like Ghana, Ivory Coast, Senegal etc. But recently Malaysia became a real hotspot for Nigerian scams. There is a huge Nigerian cell operating out of Malaysia, targeting mostly Asian women. Please keep in mind: all these white engineers supposedly from the UK but appearing in Malaysia, with awful spelling are in reality Nigerian scammers.

Where do scammers get their photos from? Many of their photos are taken from the modeling sites, like focushawaii, modelmayhem, newfaces, etc. Female pictures are almost always of the Internet porn models. But with male pictures, recently they started shifting from modeling pictures and mostly send pictures of ordinary men: either of their ex-victims or stolen from social networks, like MySpace, tagged, or from Facebook. Please visit our new picture blog, Scamdigger, to see if a pic in question has been known to be used in scams.

You should always keep in mind: The photos you see on the scammers' profiles ARE NOT the actual faces of people who are scamming you! It is very important to understand that you are NOT looking at the photos of scammers. Those are photos of innocent people scammers use, and in a way those people are victims, too. To see what scammers look like in reality, please check our hall of shame, Scammers 4 real.

The scammers have many faces. Not only do they frequently change names, email addresses, and photos, but they may list themselves on different dating sites as being of a different gender, race, age, location, and sexual orientation. Sometimes it's the opposite: Many scammers may simultaneously use the photos of the same person, like for example the images of this poor guy. It looks like half of Nigeria is using his photos.

This page is just a brief overview, sort of a doorway to our major mega-site:

Romance scam. Please visit Romancescam for more info, photo galleries, and huge forum with over 38, 000 members. Submit your scammer report there, read other victims' stories, research your scammer and educate yourself how not to fall a victim!

http://www.datingnmore.com/fraud/scam_blacklist.htm

Note: Most of Chapter 10 was derived from the internet

CHAPTER 11

SYNOPSIS

Final note: The real Uwe Hubetus is really located in Germany and is of German descent. I was told he is alive and well and around the age of fifty-eight years old at the time of this writing—and still a handsome devil (I threw that part in). This is Uwe Hubertus:

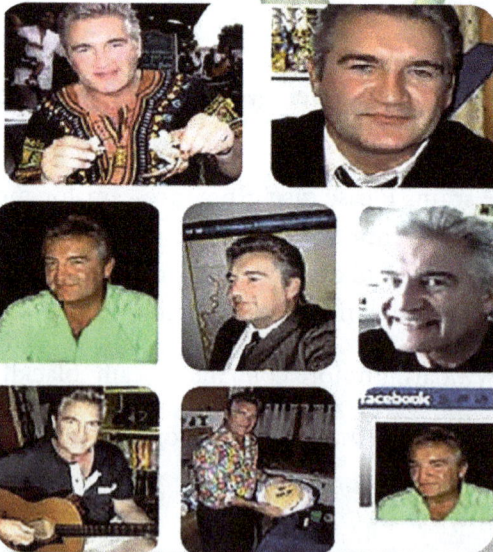

This is the most used face by scammers—and I can understand why.

This is the picture of John or whoever the real John may be. I still haven't found the real man who belongs to these pictures. I wish I knew. I liked the picture at the desk the best because his hair was all mussed up. Why am I including these pictures? In case you find him somewhere on the web with another name. IF you do, he isn't real UNLESS you see him in PERSON. Both of these men are very handsome, and it is very understandable why scammers use their pictures. Plus, their faces have an aura of honesty. Too bad the faces behind these faces aren't honest.

I actually thought this picture was real. But after I learned about the doctoring of the pictures, please note the hands. The real person is there, but the hands and the ID are inserted. I originally thought he was holding the ID closer to the camera so I could see it better, but when I scrutinized it, I was wrong.

John and his son seemed and appeared that they had the purest kind of love between a boy and his father and for the picture and the real people in it—it is, but for me? NOPE. This is the boy I worried about and the main reason I gave to the scammer what I gave. I wanted him to be safe and sound. I worried day and night for his health and wellbeing. Plus, I did for his father as well. I could not see that kind face being tortured or, worse, killed in front of his son.

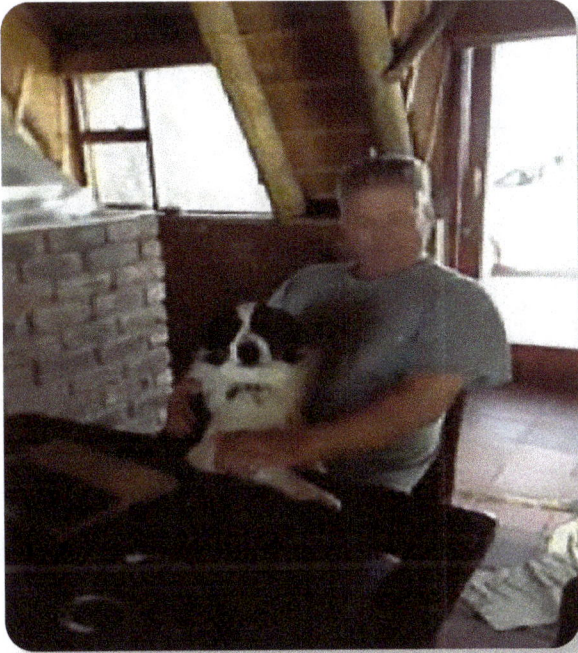

Picture of John and their dog, which I was told was taken in his sons room

Picture of John's home, which his lawyer sent to me

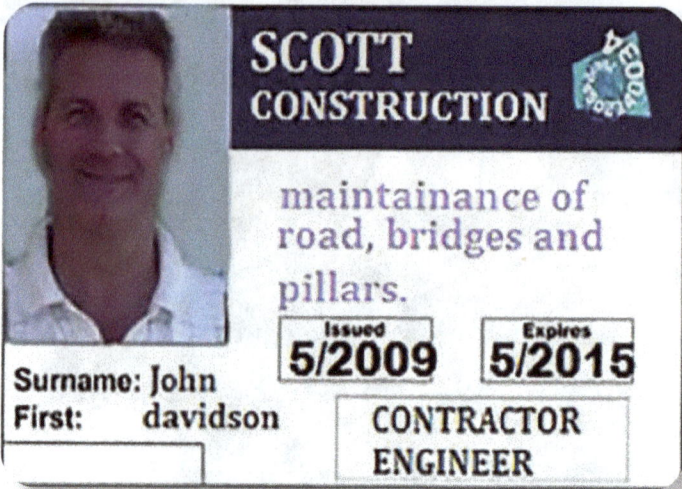

John's ID for Scott Construction but note the surname and the first name were swapped. I did notice it, but somehow I shrugged it off. It didn't seem to be an important issue at the time. Now looking back on it...

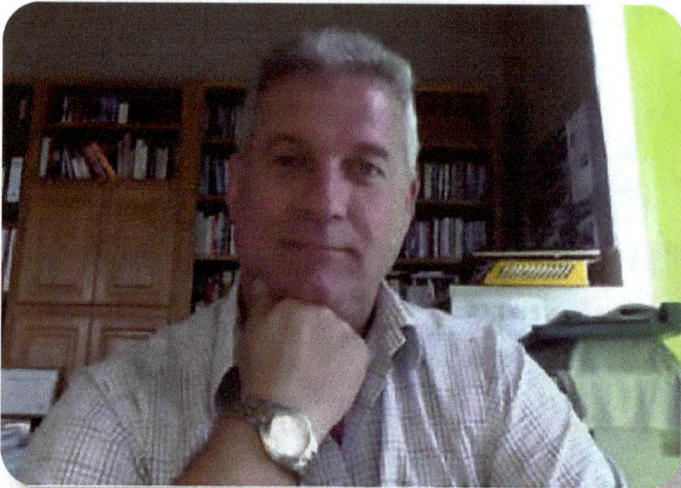

Just another picture of John, and from this file he looked like he really did have his own business with the printer, books in the bookcase, etc.

Worksite pictures

Overturned equipment that John claimed killed the Muslim worker

Pictures of worksite

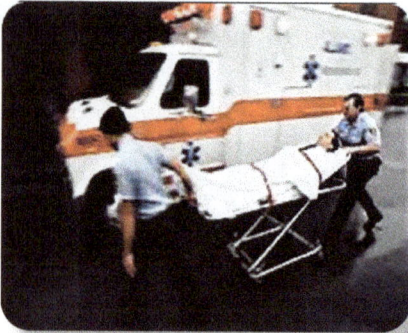
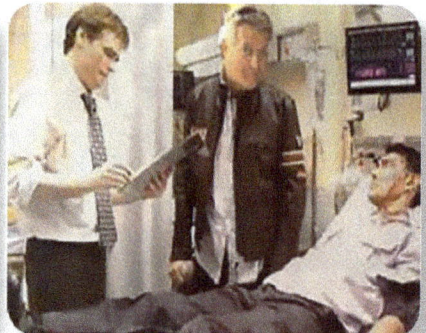

Pictures of the man's accident and then the hospital. I am noticing only now that the picture of John could have had the head inserted. I did ask why he was looking ahead and not at the man, and his response was he was looking at the nurse, who was taking the picture, because she was having trouble taking it.

Dinner in Germany

John took this picture and told me it was his breakfast in Germany. I remember telling him that I was glad I was not having breakfast there. I couldn't decipher half of the contents. But now that I look at it differently, it looks like a glass of wine by the breakfast. John did tell me he had a weakness for wine—but for breakfast?

This picture above is John working on the ship. He seemed really happy and content in this picture. This was when Kelvin got him the contract in Nigeria. BUT again, upon looking at it differently, this picture could have been altered as well by inserting a head on a body. I wish I knew who this man really is.

Picture of John outside the church located in Germany. I'm not sure if the picture was doctored or not. Face could be inserted.

Lastly, pictures of me. . .

The picture that started this whole thing, which was taken eleven years ago, and I have since removed it.

Pictures I took this year to show recent pictures and actually sent, unknowingly, to the scammers. Just in case you see my pictures other than with my own name.

My mistake was taking these pictures this year and sending them to scammers. Don't do this—please don't.

CHAPTER 12

LAST CHAPTER

This is the last chapter of my book. Remember I was still trying to keep the scammers talking so the government would respond to my request but sadly they never did. This is the response from John the first scammer as referenced in the first chapter. The book was being printed as this conversation was happening. Remember he was jailed.

I told him I was sick and couldn't do anything to assist him. Now the emails continue. They never give up. Your needs and wants will never be of importance to them. So please remember that. There are two ways to read his emails. You can read that this man is distraught and really needs assistance… OR… you can read it as someone pressuring you to give him monies and pulling out all cards, so you give him monies and has no interest in you at all but only for the almighty dollar… Unfortunately, it will always be the latter.

John's email to me on October 25, 2014. This email is precious… pretending to care about me but talking about how long he has been in jail.

My love its been a week i have not read from you, have you abandoned me honey, i am so worried, how is your health, i am so scared, even if you hate me i still love you so much, am i going to end the year in jail, please at least write me so i know your decision and please tell me you are better now, i love you honey.

My email to John on October 27. I wrote this to try and stop the requests for monies so I told him they took my phone away so I would not be stressed out.

I will get my phone sometime next week if all goes well... they said I have been very stressed out causing me health issues and possible heart attack... I have been so worried about you and Michael and then with Richmond not assisting when he had the money and opportunity... How is Micheal I need to know...He is causing me the greatest stress... Hope all is ok with you as well... Love ya... I don't have access to this computer so just know I still care...

John's email in response on November 1. Now in the above email I did state what was wrong with me stating it was stress but again it is about him and his son :

Honey its been days since i heard from you, how is your health, you never told me the sickness you had that kept you in the hospital for close to 3 months, what is happening as the years draws to an end i get so worried, will i see the end of the year in prison with our son very sick, please i need to hear from you ,do not be afraid, tell me the truth, it is better i know than i keep hoping, i know you have tried so much for me, i love you so much, but please tell me what is my hope on my current situation, i wait to read from you, muahhh

My response on the same day stating I was stress:

Keep this up and they will take my phone again... extreme anxiety causing me a possible heart attack due to worry about u and micheal... if micheal was at least doing better...

John's response on November 2. John still having trouble understanding stress and again it is not me he is worried about:

Honey you have said this for 3 months now, please tell me what is the name of your sickness, i am worried about you, please understand me, i need to know my hope honey, i love you so much and i will always love you

John's continues to email even though I stopped. Email written November the 10, 2014... and again the email is about how he is suffering.

Honey how are you, its been weeks since i last heard from you, you do not even want to talk with me anymore, it is so strange you could behave this way, i am suffering here and you allow me to suffer, heaven's know i truly loved you, you have hurt me so badly, i wish you the best

My Response on November 11, 2014:

It's all about you always... and it hasn't been weeks... I need healing time and you refuse to give it to me... I can't help you if I need help myself... UNDERSTAND? YOU are the one hurting yourself and Michael... not me... I am having the results of too much stress... If I cannot relieve the stress I could have a heart attack and then you would be right and I will be dead... SO LET ME HAVE THE REST THEY SUGGEST... The more you write the more stress you give me... I need rest... let me have it or you will be right...

John's reply and kind of curt:

Suit yourself,i have suffered so much already,rest as much as you can okay

My reply same day:

Suit yourself? Really? you have suffered not me or Michael just you? REALLY? your attention should be on your son... I could have gotten him out a long time ago and he would be in the states...

John's response: same day and again it is about his needs:

How can you get Michael out when you have refused to help, for 7 months now i have stayed here in jail and you dare to tell me you have been sick, even if you will let me die at least not Michael, now I have Michael hospital bills to pay before he can be released and you tell me the doctors say this and that, that is all a lie, i know you are okay and not sick, stop lying about you been sick okay, just get my Michael out of here, you can leave me to suffer if you wish but please get Michael out of here

My response same day as I am getting tired of his whining:

Plus, you have no idea what I have gone through... I don't whine like someone i know...

John's response on November 23, 2014

Honey how are you, i do not read your emails anymore, are you okay, please let me know what is going on

My response on November 24, 2014

You gave me time to recoup... so thank you... I need to go back to work so all should go better

John's response on December 1, 2014 and of course he is blaming me for his son's death.

How are you, i know you have abandoned us here but i want to say thank you for all you did for us, i love you so much, happy new month, i miss you so much, so you know we lost Micheal, he died of cancer due to inadequate treatment, life has taught me a bitter lesson, once again thank you

My response on December 1, 2014

Thanks for at least informing me of Micheal... I am so sorry this all happened... IF only you never went to Germany... I am deeply saddened and have not abandoned you in any way shape or form. I need to make some sales in order to get some money and this is the slow time of the year for real estate... All I can say is to hang in there for me... OK? Love you more than words can ever say...

John's response on December 4, 2014 and again he is feeling sorry for his losses:

am crying as i write you now, i have lost all my family, i lost my mother, my ex-wife and now my bundle of joy, Michael is gone, honey will i lose you too, who do i have now in this world, i am just here amd do not know when i will leave here, i do not know if to believe you will help me or you are just fooling me, i feel you are fed up with me and do not know how to say it so rather you allow me suffer here in pains. Honey how much can you come up with so i know how to plead with this people here and get my freedom, i love you honey and i miss you so much, honey i do not want to die here

My response on December 5

John... I know you have suffered and so have I... You still have me, and you still have your father...and you have Richmond. Instead of centering on what you don't have try centering on what you do have... U left me in a hole and with Michael being ill and you in jail took a toll on me and I lost a lot of work due to worry. I have to make up the loss. I owe for my real estate license and RE fees which are a lot... I have some makeup to do and I need to make some sales... this is the bad time of the year. Nothing I can do to increase sales... Blame Richmond... you and Michael could have gotten out months ago if it wasn't for him not sending me the funds... I have no idea what you want me to do to speed anything up... It has to take its toll... it just does... I would like it if you quit whining all the time. If you keep making me worried, I will probably have to go back to the doctor which I don't want to do... so PLEASE let me do my thing... I know you have it rough... I know... trust me I do and I am trying to get you out as I already said... I have no idea what you think I can do... I have no magic wand... I gave you my entire life savings... I have no money and you left me in a hole in March... You caused yourself to be in this mess... Why you placed your money in the bank and why you didn't give it to Richmond until you came back to the US is beyond me... Why you went to Germany is still beyond me... but it is what it is until I can drum up the money to get you out... but I will have to go there to get you out... I have everyone looking to see where the money is going... because of the large amount of monies I already gave to Richmond... I didn't forget about you... You never told me exactly when Michael passed away... can you tell me? Have to go to bed to get up early to see who is wanting to buy or sell property... Good Night... and try to rest... ok?

John's response on December 10 and again asking for help and his needs:

Honey how are you, i know you have read my messages but you did not reply, hope all is well with you, this is my last message to you, if you wish to help me okay, if you do not wish to help, no problem either, just be safe and take good care of yourself, love you

My response on December 11:

You have to understand that after I left John I have more money worries than you can ever imagine and I have the FBI, Interpole and CIA also watching me for all the large sums of monies I already gave... Plus trying to make sales to make ends meet and then also earn enough to get you out of there. I am working all the time and don't have much tome to respond when you need me too. I barely have time to breathe... So I have to ask you to be patient. I had someone who was going to give me the funds but he too got into trouble so no help from that aspect either. I have been trying... but I don't want to burden you with all the things I have been going thru since you have so many issues of your own. Just know that I am trying... plus my PC connection isn't the best where I am and I have trouble logging on... It goes on and off with the connections... Please just know I haven't forgotten... and please be patient...

John's response December 14:

Honey i love you, please write me so i know how you are

My response on December 15:

Im ok... just that weekends is my busy time... I showed homes this morning and open house this afternoon... people wanted to buy at open house but waiting for money from a job injury... oh well... nothing I can do about that

John's response December 19. This is another precious email when he asks for my credit card and all my info. I guess he didn't think that I could use my own credit card. It's always the monies. I know he's scamming me:

Honey how are you, i have not heard from you in days now,i hope you are okay, honey i have suffered so much here, i have a friend of mine who i know will help me but i need to write him on Christianmingle.com, when we left school we created a group profile so we could always get in touch with each other, honey i need to write him Asap, so he knows what i am going through and helps me, but my subscription on the site has expired, can you give me your visa card details, like Name, card number, phone number, card expiry date, city, state, security code, zip code of your card so i can subscribe on the site and write him, honey it costs very little to subscribe, please do this for me so i can contact him, love you so much, just send me this details so i can subscribe and contact him.

My response same day. Why would anyone give their credit card info knowing that you are being scammed:

Credit cards are all maxed out from when I had to get phones, and extract monies... Sorry no can do but I am sure your attorney can give that to you... I am so sorry but my funds are maxed out and tried numerous times to tell you that... ALL credit cards are maxed out... I literally have nothing left... That is what makes getting you out so hard to do... but several people want to write offers... so let's see how that goes... ok?

John's response same day:

Honey thank you so much for your kind words, i know i have caused you the greatest pain in the world but i will also bring you the greatest joy you ever felt in life, they say good things come to those who wait, you have wait and once i leave here and can access my account i will shower you the year here, i cry when i remember Michael, i cry most because i wasnt able to bury my son, nor do i know where he was buried, i was locked up in jail, but i love you and i am so grateful, i know if truly you are telling me the truth one day i will leave here, but if you have your mind made up not to help me any further, know i still love you so much, please send me a photo of you so i can admire you whenever i have access online. Send me the photo honey.

My response on December 20

John,

   Talk to Richmond and see if he can give you the funds to reconnect with your buddy...

Hopefully he has a few hundred on him to help out a friend.

John's response same day... Of course his lawyer, his friend is always busy or on vacation but can never give him any monies. He has money for vacations and trips but not to give his friend.

Richmond has travelled out for Christmas, i cannot get in touch with him anymore till he returns honey

My response same day:

If he had money to travel then he has it oi help u get connected to your friend.

John's response same day. Always a reason that someone else cannot give money but it's always me to get him out of trouble by giving money:

He has travelled out of the states, his cards are all blocked and to make matters worst he is offline even on email, i cannot reach him until he comes back.

John's email Christmas Eve. What an email to give someone you love an email like the one below.

Honey compliments of the season to you, it hurts me so badly i am saying this in phone to you while i should have been with you. Honey i need your help asap to save my home, i just got a notice from the Tax office and Environmental Care/Facilities unit in my home, they have urged me to pay my tax and maintenance due before the week runs out or my home will be sealed, honey you know i have been here for long and i have not paid for a very long time, please i need you to help me, the fee accumulating since April is $2600, please get back to me honey, i need your help so our home do not get sealed, get back to me immediately you ser this message. Love you

My final response to John on March 15th 2015:

I wrote this to you a long time ago and now I am sending it... The airline ticket did it especially the airline ticket person with a Nigerian accent... I do have free tickets which are issued by American Airlines.

You are the lowest of the life form ever... and one hell of a son of a bitch...
Dare to wish me a Merry Christmas... you are the scum of all scums..
Not only did you take all my monies under a disguise of being
John Davidson. You killed a little boy off who is probably still
alive and enjoying the holiday for the sake of getting all my funds.
You are the sickest human alive. You are worse than a bloodsucking leech.
I knew you were lying since you were jailed.
I truly believed in you. You wear someone else's face as a guide to get
monies. You select an innocent face and a picture of a sweet little boy.
IF I ever see the real you I will spit in your face for all the headache's
you have caused me and for all the tears I have shed worrying about
someone who doesn't exist.
YOU ARE SCUM! PIECE OF FILTH! DON'T EVEN HAVE THE
GUTS TO USE YOUR OWN FACE OR NAME ... I truly loved you
with all my heart and you ripped it out of my chest time and time
again... MAY YOU DIE A MOST PAINFUL DEATH EVER... Try
using your own name and face for a change of pace instead of hiding
like a coward... PIECE OF SHIT!!!!!

John's response once again and final response on March 30, 2015. Scammers never give up. They just don't:

You dare say all this to me and call me SCUM, i wish you the best, i
will fight my way home and when i come home i must search for you and
pay you all your money

By the way, I never saw or heard from John again and never wanted to... I kept him on the hook for a long time wanting the IC3 or Interpol or FBI to respond and no one ever has and the year is now 2022. Sad but true.

The strange part is I did hear from Scamwatch? June 9, 2019. Below is their response. Did it help in any way? NO! Scamwatch is run by the Australian Competition and Consumer Commission (ACCC). It provides information to consumers and small businesses about how to recognize, avoid and report scams.

It is legit per the internet. But why after all this time that passed would they even email me???

Thank you for reporting this scam

Your submission ID: accc-scamwatch:571682

Your report is important to the ACCC as this information assists us in monitoring scam trends and taking action where appropriate, including to educate the public on new or emerging scams. The ACCC doesn't respond to reports made via this form due to the high volume received.

If you need advice about how to deal with a scam, please visit the Scamwatch website.

You can also follow @Scamwatch.gov on Twitter and subscribe to Scamwatch radar alerts to keep up to date with the latest scams.

Submitted on 10 Jun 2019 - 3:38 am

Would you be willing to share your story?:	Yes, I'm willing to share my story to raise awareness of scams. I am happy for the ACCC to contact me to discuss it further.
Do you give permission for your scam report (including any personal information you provide) to be shared with other government agencies?:	Yes

About the scam

What type of scam is it?:	Dating & romance
How were you contacted by the scammer?:	Internet
Which website were you using?:	Facebook
Are you willing to share this report with Facebook Ireland Limited (Facebook)?:	No
When were you first contacted?:	09/06/2014
What losses did you suffer?:	Financial

Amount lost:	150 000.00
Lost via:	Other payment method
Payment method details:	Transfer
Briefly describe the scam:	My loss is a lost cause. It happened many years ago, but I wrote a book called WOW! Scammed or not scammed. I wrote it to help people to understand and identify the writings of scammers and some of the ways to identify them. Nothing helped me back then n I wanted to inform people that sometimes they work in groups n children are sometimes used as they were in my case. Plus, the monies don't always get transferred to overseas but to American bank accounts as well. I want the people to know how to identify and to spend their monies on themselves and not imaginary people. But getting the word out is hard. I was wondering if you have any ideas. I don't have the monies to actively promote the book. I have a few copies that I can give away if anyone needs it. But if you can help that would be great. The agencies back then did nothing not sure if they are any better today but once scammed you are a target for the scammers for repeat business so to speak and sometimes, I still get threats. But it is what it is. They are quite good at what they do. I have spent my money on some promotional items, and it isn't just in the states but international problem. Dorrance Publishing has given it to bookstores, but they don't place all newly written books on their shelves but is available thru them and bookstores as well and as I said I have a few that I can give away. I'm soooo tired of scammers.

About the scammer

Scammer's name: John Davidson

Why am I including all these emails after all this time? Well, the answer is simple. I want you to know that it is always about the scammer wants and needs and not yours. You could be dying of some illness and they will still make it about themselves. You need to know how they write and the guilt they will try and put on you for not being able to assist them. Plus, it is the end of the story. But other stories have blossomed such as someone trying to contact me from Interpol but that too was a scammer... Baseline? Be very careful of your conversations with people you do not know. HANG UP! Being able to identify a scammer is the key to stopping scammers.

www.ingramcontent.com/pod-product-compliance
Lightning Source LLC
Chambersburg PA
CBHW060241030426
42335CB00014B/1562